...And...

By

Isabel Adonis

Black Bee Books Ltd.

First Published in Great Britain in 2022 by
Black Bee Books Ltd
Bryn Heulog
Talley
Llandeilo
Wales SA19 7YH
Copyright © Isabel Adonis 2022

Cover Image © Isabel Adonis
Cover Design © Huw Francis

ISBN: 978-1-913853-10-5 (Paperback)
ISBN: 978-1-913853-11-2 (eBook)

www.blackbeebooks.wales

Acknowledgements

My book is dedicated to:

Yemaya Carida
Catherine Alice
Morgan Joe
Samuel

Dedication

to bob

Chapter One

In which my mother says she wants to be buried in rags and sacking – and is not.

And my mother always said that when she died she wanted to be buried face down in rags and sacking. Many times she said: "When I die, I want to be buried dressed in rags and sacking, face down in the earth." Nothing else, she wanted nothing else, so that even in her death she could deny desire, and she never wanted anything in life or death because for her, the worst thing was to want. And she said: "I don't want, I don't know how to want," so that when it came to mentioning her end, she wanted to not want. She never saw of course that her dying wish was a contradiction, how it contained, in her denial, the very want she was avoiding, and that behind every denial of want was the want; the want she did not want. And she lived her whole life like this, negatively, and perfectly confident at the same time, not of what she wanted but of all that she did not want.

It was amusing, though she was perfectly serious; it was frightening too, since it demanded that I as her daughter would have to act on her wishes, and it was easier to ignore her. Her desire was to extend beyond death itself and this wish seemed to say more about her than almost any other thing. She said: "I don't want any fuss made over me, I don't want to be a problem to anyone, I don't want a coffin, I don't want a church service." All contradictions, and her list would be endless, an impossible list of not-wants.

As much as she hated wanting and believed that she could not want, she hated religion even while it was at the centre of her life. "The Lord is my Shepherd I shall not want," she said quietly to herself; and religion and desire were incompatible. There it was, imprinted on her brain as her earliest memory; wanting and religion did not go together, and if her life was to be religious practice there was no wanting.

1

Perhaps this was why she saw that they, the religious ones, wanted too much and therefore the Lord was not their shepherd, as the Lord was her shepherd. Perhaps she saw their hypocrisy but didn't see her own reflection in them, for she sought always to be purer and yet still purer and she would always have to be lower, and therefore higher, in her relation to the world. She sought humility and she talked of virtue and smallness and she believed she was it; she spoke of those who stole virtue and she would turn every stone until she received God's grace, even if it didn't come to her until old age, like some biblical hero, and her life would be transformed by his intervention.

She would be transformed through religious baptism. She prayed for this; the life she was ceaselessly wanting, and while not wanting it she would search the good book – Y Beibl, which is 'the bible' in Welsh. But her liberation never came, not even in death or before it, and neither did her dying wish that she should be buried in this non-conformist way.

And my mother, Catherine she was called, had no shortage of rags and sacking; she had been collecting them over a long period of time; she collected large open weaved sacks, some were plain and some had print on them and some were just plain dirty but she didn't mind dirt. Holding them up to the light she would examine the size and the weave and if they were crumpled she would carefully and lovingly wash each one. She had a very loving way about her in everything she did; and after washing it, she would dry it on a washing line and air it until it was quite dry and then store it for her inevitable death. Once she even took out a bradawl, a small tool for pushing small cut strips of cloth through the weave, to make one of her sacks into a mat. And everything she did was for the glory of God, and sewing was a prayer and a meditation to Him, which had its own rewards, not here on earth but in heaven.

She said rags and sacking to demonstrate her humility, her smallness, her virtue, and because she loved cloth more than wood and sewing more than carpentry. Carpentry was for men and she was not a man; her dealings with wood were restricted to the collecting of twigs for her coal fire. When she lived in Bangor, on the mountain and close to trees and woodland, she bought a red bow saw and a small dark red handled chopping knife to cut these small pieces of wood. Sometimes she could be seen sawing up a long piece of ash and she would be standing balancing a long branch and aiming to not fall since she stood on a slope. There was an ash tree behind her home and sometimes she would drag smaller branches into her hillside garden and she would cut them again into twigs. But when it came to any consideration of death and dying it wasn't wood she thought of, it was cloth. And besides, she wanted to resist them, those men that made all kinds of rules about this and that, and every type of human activity, and especially in matters of the human heart. She would express herself through the softness of rags and sacking.

She was a kind of expert on cloth and especially old cloth, it excited her in a sensual way; the smell, the weight, the feel, the weave, the dye and the colour reminded her of a lost skin, of lost love and lost intimacy; her mother's long dark skirt, her beautifully stitched and starched white cotton blouse with full sleeves, the little buttons at the cuff, her father, Johnny Willy's wool suit, his bow tie and his tweed cloth cap. She told me years ago a tale of going upstairs as a child, to the attic and seeing the old clothes which her grandparents had worn and she hadn't just remembered it, she had absorbed it into her child mind and her child body, and there it had stayed as some hidden language. She told me how she remembered the black and white clothes and how that was an image she had to live by, like the very skin she was in and she would live with those colours of black and white, an image that would determine her destiny, an image to stand under and live by. Black and white, black and white bound her to a past, which sustained her present.

She never said anything about her own mother's face, her mother's hair or her mother's skin or her mother's ways; except that she died when she was six and behind her mother there was nothing and before her mother there was nothing and around her mother there was nothing. And she scarcely talked, as if all that had passed was frozen, although it was still right there. She just said: "She died when I was six." And when I was very young I thought that when my mother died my eldest sister, Janice would become my mother and then when she died my sister, Evelyn would be my mother and then it would be my turn to be my mother, but it didn't turn out like that.

Soon after my father left my mother, she busied herself collecting cloth. We had left Llandudno; we had had to leave because the bank manager had insisted that my mother sell the house, because my father had left us in debt, a debt that wouldn't have mattered if he'd still been working in Africa, but he wasn't. I can remember he earned about two thousand pounds then and it was called a salary, and this salary included free travel to Africa and the other benefits like boarding-school fees and something called superannuation. The bank manager called her in and he told her. He said: "You will have to have a second mortgage on your home," and of course she didn't want a second mortgage because she knew she could not pay the first, and the bank manager knew that too.

The debt meant that she had to leave the first house, which was called Beiteel. And it was the first house, she, my mother, had ever had and a house which was never a home or a haven or a place of comfort or anything like that, though she wanted it to be. And she had to leave a life, which at one time had almost given her a certain privilege and a certain status. And then she was not going up in the world as people say, and there was no more paid travel or boarding-school fees, nor was there anymore any superannuation, not that my mother was particularly interested in that.

And soon after he left we went to live in Bangor, which was just up the coast from Llandudno, and Bangor was a university town, there was a university on the hill overlooking the town. And it was closer to the mountains where she could buy a cheaper house and pay off the debt she owed the bank. Then she began to fill her time with collecting clothes from a charity shop, which was called Oxfam; there was only one charity shop at the time in Bangor but later there were many more. And when there were more she went to Oxfam and all the others.

Sometimes she had arguments with the women who ran the shop and she would return home, full of defiance and hurt and outrage, and it was their goodness she despised and their monopoly on goodness, the way they had a chance to see all the clothes before she did, the way they wouldn't let her negotiate for clothes as she would have preferred. Like an African woman she felt it her right to do that – to barter and bargain. She was poor and she could never understand why it was the poor who supported the poor. I can remember her adding up each penny spent in a little notebook she had bought at Woolworth's, and accounting for all that she spent. And she would pay her bills in instalments long before this idea caught on.

And after a long time she saved eighty pounds in this way and she deposited it at the Halifax Building Society and she was very pleased with herself and proud of her abilities. She didn't work outside the home, because that was my father's role and now he was gone and he had taken that life with him; the life she had worked for. She couldn't stand the isolation, for she was a sociable sort, though she was not one for social niceties.

But regardless of all her disagreements at the charity shop she kept on buying and collecting. She collected cardigans, jumpers, waistcoats with fancy buttons, wool coats for children, wool coats for grown ups, silk dressing gowns for men and for women, silk printed dresses, hats, Kangol berets in all colours, hats in hat boxes and hats not in hat boxes, leather gloves and dressing-up gloves of delicate leather, little lacy tops and silk scarves, fox furs and beaver furs and fur coats, pleated skirts and tweed skirts and silk and Scottish kilts and pyjama cases. And each item was lovingly washed or brushed, altered or mended and assigned a place in her bedroom, which was soon bursting like a well-stocked charity shop. The berets were steamed and thoroughly cleaned and she wore them with pride.

And she collected small things like buttons and lengths of ribbons and braid and broken brooches and expensive pens that didn't work and endless pairs of reading glasses (for the frames) and old leather bags and satchels of different kinds. She liked old things and worn things and all those things which were unloved and required attention. And her room was bursting with treasures and there was no room there, though every single thing was ordered and perfectly clean, for if anything had a small stain she would douse it with lemon juice or iron it with brown paper or brush it until it was clean. And her room was intimate and cosy and comfortable and it was clean and interesting and there was a whole world of opportunity and wonder there.

The bedroom suite was a pale wood and had been bought second hand from Auntie Maggie, or rather Auntie Maggie's son, David, for seventeen pounds. It was the first and only bedroom suite she had. Auntie Maggie had come to the house in her usual way and said that she had something for my mother. She said: "David is selling a bedroom suite and it is such a bargain." And my mother put so many clothes in the wardrobe, it could not be adequately closed, and she jammed the door with a rolled up bit of paper and forced it closed. She had a pair of purple curtains on the window which looked back on the mountain, that I had bought for her from Pollecoffs Bangor – an old fashioned shop where receipts were always written out by hand with a pen and ink, and the money went on odd journeys around the shop in a lift and a brass container, and men spoke graciously of service.

Her dressing table was covered in all kinds of interesting

things, used lipstick cases, old perfume bottles, empty talcum powder pots, empty tin tubs of Nivea and empty tin tubs of Boots face cream which was like Nivea, a tube of pink Germolene and a pot of lanolin, a home made silk bag, old safety pins, and boxes of unused Morny soaps. There was always Johnson's baby powder, a tall white container whose smell of babies filled the air.

For darning she had a mushroom shaped wooden tool over which she stretched a woollen sock for repair: she would unravel the broken threads and begin creating a new warp and weft with a long darning needle and fine wool, kept on a card. She would be sat hunched over by a window straining towards the light as if in prayer, and darning was prayer itself. She could do this for socks and she could do this for stockings and she knew how to make a proper patch for a cotton sheet and how to make a bodice for a girl's dress and how to make women's underwear and how to make an ankle on a pair of knitted socks. She knew how to make a girl's dress and a pair of trousers without a pattern, how to make every kind of skirt and cut it on the bias or how to make a pleat. And she seemed to know how to do everything to do with clothes as if it were a language she knew.

And shoes. She collected all kinds of shoes, flat brown shoes, leather brogues with proper stitching along the soles and not moulded, shoes with great long laces made of leather and some had laces not made of leather, high heeled shoes in patent leather which she would never wear, purple suede shoes and pink shoes, shoes with bars and shoes with buckles, stuffed with balls of scrunched up newspaper and shoe horns. And once she bought me dancers' shoes by Anello and Davide and I loved those shoes and I had two pairs, a red pair and a black pair.

The insides of shoes would be cleaned with a damp cloth (and not wet), moistened with Dettol, she believed in Dettol, just like the cross itself, after which she would put one shoe next to the other shoe, as if they were twins and place them under the bed.

She must have had about forty pairs of shoes of which she only wore one or two pairs and not one of them new, and they were pushed under her bed along with other treasures for the life she might lead or might have led. There was a large piece of sandstone, which my father had taken from an archaeological dig at Meroë in the Sudan; that is what she said anyway. And a rolled up print which the artist Roger Hilton had given my father; she had some manuscripts and a box of green tiles which had been made for a coffee table designed by my father and based on a rubbing from an Egyptian tomb. The table was never made, though for a time it was there in the house, just put together roughly. I always felt it very bad luck to keep that piece of sandstone, for I feared it would act as a curse on her life and his, to remove something sacred, like when Lord Caernarvon raided the Egyptian tomb. I had read about Lord Caernarvon in a book on archaeology by Stuart Piggot that my father had given me.

Under her bed and in her wardrobe and on top of her wardrobe and all about her room were the clothes of a life she no longer had and would no longer have that she couldn't let go. It was as if no person could live here in this well ordered, clean, darned and intimate room; an intimacy so close and so suffocating, and a resourcefulness carried to an extreme degree and she believed that she didn't have anything because somehow all of this did not count, which was also true.

Chapter Two

A day in which the sea was grey and the river was grey and the sky was grey and the cloud was grey and the slate was grey.

She was named Catherine Alice Hughes and she was born in October 1917 and she died in February 2001, aged eighty four, when the earth was cold and hard and the days bleak and grey. A day when the trees in the woods were bare and the river was low and the water ran down the valley slowly. I called her Nainie back then, a name I started using when my sons were small; it means 'Granny' in Welsh. Before that I used to call her Ma. I never called her Catherine Alice, which was her name. My father called her Catherine when he was angry or insistent. I don't know if he called her Catherine in love, but I never heard it. Father called her Catherine – he said "Catherine" the way he called "Joseph" who was our servant in Africa. So death meant no more Nainie, or Ma, or mother or mam (she was never called mam), or mummy, or Catherine.

My sister, Janice, phoned me and she said: "Nainie is dead," or: "Ma is dead," or something like that. And then I said: "I would like to see her one last time." And she said she would come up to Bethesda to collect the girls and me; she said: "I'll be up in an hour to collect you and the girls and take you to Llandudno to see her." And she said: "Ma died peacefully."

I was in bed and it was a Sunday I think. She had said: "I'll come and collect you, I'm going over to Llandudno soon, and I'll pick you up on the way." I didn't feel sad at all, but it was sad: I was in bed alone and I got up and opened the curtains, which were made in the design of a patchwork quilt. It had many colours and many different scraps and some of the squares I had printed on with paint and I noticed the way the light came through the squares of colour; I walked over the wooden floor and I looked at the huge trees and the river. The River Ogwen was grey water gently tumbling round the grey rocks and the pieces of slate. The slate in the water gave it a certain colour, and the river was passing under the bridge, and the bridge was grey and the water went right past the huge rock that was under the bridge and away round the bend of the river. I looked down as far as my eye could see; all the way to the special island in the bend of the river where the water went around and I noticed the trees in the woods were bare and the ground was hard and unyielding, and no children had yet gone over the bridge and into the park to play on the swings or the slide that morning as they did on Sunday mornings.

I went up the stairs and along the long wooden corridor and called my eldest daughter, Catherine, to get up, and I said: "Get up, Baba, get up Catherine, Nainie has died and we are going to see her one last time." I called her by her two names, both Baba and Catherine, as if I were simultaneously calling her father – in the Yoruba language – and Catherine, as mother. She was sleeping and she opened her eyes and I saw her black eyes and her black hair was curly; she stretched her arms behind her and she said quietly: "I'll get up now," and that is all she said. And I walked back down the corridor and looked again at the trees and the river through the window at the top of the house. I looked over to the slate mountain as I would always do and then I walked downstairs and entered Yemaya's room, who was my youngest daughter. She was asleep and I woke her and I said: "Yemaya, Nainie's died and we're going to see her for one last time, and Auntie Janice is coming to collect us in half an hour." And she awoke immediately and looked about her and her room was a hard yellow colour and above the window was a painting of a circus scene. And then I got ready to see Nainie for the last time; Nainie who was my mother, Catherine, ma, mam, though nobody ever called her that even though she was Welsh.

So Janice drove up to Bethesda where we lived back then in her Jetta, which was the name of her car, and she stood at the front door, and we were all ready, the two girls and myself. She wore a black tailored jacket, which I recognised; it was one of mine that I had given her, and I remembered clothes and their meaning and their power. I thought of my mother's clothes and the way I always had to go and smell them in her room, like they were her skin and the skin of the past, like she had done when she was a little girl. I think that's one of mine, I thought, but I didn't say it. I didn't want to talk, not that I was sad, I wasn't; and she was talking about this and that, the business of death and dying, but I wasn't really listening.

She drove out of the town called Bethesda, which is a holy name from the bible and the name of the holy pool and lots of Welsh towns have names like that and they begin with Llan which is 'church of' in Welsh. Some towns are called Llandudno and Llangefni and Llanfestiniog. I looked at the quarry men's cottages, which were so familiar to me, and they were small squares where people lived and conducted their lives, small squares in space and time. I saw all the bends in the road, which were so familiar to me and as intimate to me as were my mother's clothes: I saw Half Way Bridge and this was grey, where the river cuts down and changes course by some huge trees. The river is called the Ogwen and the valley is called the Ogwen Valley or Dyffryn Ogwen in Welsh.

The girls were in the back of the car and they were quiet, motionless even, and not chatting amongst themselves. The morning was grey, the air itself seemed grey; a grey sky touched the horizon, which was covered with a thin cloud of grey and I saw the grey water in the distance – the Straits, it is called, and further still Anglesey and Puffin Island. Puffin Island was once home to thousands of rats: I smiled when I remembered that. I had once known someone who had spent the night there or part of the night there with them. We passed through Abergwyngreg-yn and Llanfairfechan and Penmaenmawr, where there is a huge clock on the side of the mountain and where my mother had gone for short holidays from the Cartref Bontnewydd Home when she was a child and a young woman. And we passed the place where my father had stopped his car in 1955 and it was just near to the entrance of the old tunnel, near Conway, which is now called Conwy.

Then Janice drove us over the flyover at Conwy and I noticed the old bridge and I remembered it and the old Crosville bus that crossed that same bridge and how it always seemed to get stuck there, but didn't actually. We passed Deganwy and Maggie Murphy's, the chip shop, and then we went into Llandudno. She drove to the shore past all the hotels on the beach front, and alongside the promenade to near the paddling pool – the place I used to visit as a child, alone with my bike; it had always been a special and sentimental place for me, where the old ladies from Nottingham had sat making lace while they watched the little children at play. And it was a place where a young girl had been murdered, an innocent little girl. And children played there all day in the summer by the large shallow pool and the inside was painted light blue.

My mother had been in this area before: she had been at the unmarried mother's home where she had her first child: she had been here in Llandudno in 1945 and she had stayed up the Orme and worked in the Hydro Hotel, doing "war work" she called it. Her husband, Mr Coleman, had come after her with a gun. She said: "Mr Coleman came after me with a gun and he wanted me to give up my baby. He said if I didn't give up my baby then he would sue me for adultery." And then she said that a doctor had offered to have it. She had stayed up the Orme and she had had her baby at the unmarried mother's home and she had been divorced for adultery. And it was this kind of thing that made my mother heroic though nobody would ever know: she was heroic, because she had a black baby in a time when black servicemen were being executed for going with white women.

And my mother believed in honour and she carried her honour everywhere with her and amongst people who did not believe in it or anything at all. And she believed that people could be honourable and that some people were honourable. She thought that American cowboys were honourable and she said: "They are the last of the honourable men."

Having a baby back then was a terrible shame, and having a black baby was even worse of a shame: but she knew, she knew that the place for children was not in a home and she carried her shame and she carried society's shame before her and she carried it with her body and in her body, and she was not afraid, and she was honourable.

Inside the old people's home, the whole place smelled of overcooked cabbage which reminded me of my mother and Sundays at home and thinking of doing school homework and not doing it and watching Fred MacMurray on the television and I Love Lucy and Mr Ed and having a boiled egg and bread and butter for tea. I always thought the way my mother cut bread was strange because she always melted a small piece of butter on a small plate and she seemed to know just how long to soften it with her knife or under the grill before it would melt and be useless. She had a special butter knife for spreading and she would spread it so thin on a thinly cut piece of bread and she would hold the bread as if she were holding a baby to her breast.

Bread itself was religious and meaningful because it was the bread of heaven. We had cake too because I liked to make a Victoria sponge and Madeira cake with butter; occasionally I would make her a Cherry Genoa which is kind of white inside. We had two tins for making these sponges and I imagined myself as a TV cook like Fanny Craddock. I thought that it was some kind of special talent of mine. I made cake and I wanted to please my mother so that she would notice and love me.

The smell of cabbage reminded me of all of that. And I followed my sister up the mahogany stairs and behind me were my two daughters, Baba and Yemaya and they weren't talking and we passed a stained glass window, and the stairs turned around and about and we walked up to the room to where my mother lay in a room behind a mahogany door.

She was a white woman: my mother was a white woman and she lay dead on a single bed before me, which was turned away from the window along the side of a wall and it faced a dressing table. My eldest sister was there and two of my younger sisters called Charlotte and Beatrice, and Phoebe was there, which was Charlotte's daughter. It was awkward because I had left them, and I had left mother. I had left them just like father did because I was father even though I didn't know him. And a white woman with short white hair lay on the bed and each of her daughters was not white. It was awkward because I didn't know them any more; I wanted to be free as father had done and that meant I had to give them up and I had had to go away, because I was father. Not that it was a matter of choice, it was something in life that was going to happen and one of those things that was already written for me, and it was just the way it was. I was father, and father had to go away and I had to go away and father had to search to be free and I had to search to be free.

She was dead and I didn't have a mother anymore; I didn't have a mother any more before that time either, but now she was dead and her body looked like a young girl, as though her whole life of being a mother had already gone out of her body before she died. Someone had painted her nails rose red to make her nice and I remembered the problems she always had with her nails which were always breaking and the sores she sometimes had and her sitting in a chair with her sore fingers soaking in warm water and Dettol to make them better. And sometimes she would quietly paint them with whatever nail polish was around, and then she would curl her fingers towards her and briefly look at them. But there was nothing really glamorous about her nails, which were short and round and her hands were small, and her nails often had splits in.

She had worked so hard in her life in a physical way, and when

14

she was about sixty-seven her right arm just curled up in a strange way and then was continuously bent at the elbow. I went with her to the old C and A hospital in Bangor and the doctor couldn't believe what had happened to her arm: I did not know what had happened either and a doctor came and took a photo of it and said he had never seen anything like it before.

I sat down on the chair and looked at her closed eyes, her nose – it was quite straight, and her small thin mouth – it was quite thin. Her chest beneath her nightie seemed flat, like a girl's, and the body and her womb, which had born five daughters, was all dead – but it seemed just like a girl's. Her arms were thin, and her pink skin was no longer pink, but quite white, like white paste. All the life had gone out of her, all that trying she had always talked about; trying was important to her and she said, she always said: "All you can do is try." But this was the end to her trying, and it was no use and she always said it. This was the end of her and the end of trying and this was the end to the heavy burden that was herself and to all the work of being a mother.

And the ones who were caring for her in the last days had brought her here, to Llandudno and I liked to call the place, "Ar Lan y Mor" which meant "by the seaside" in Welsh. My mother was Welsh. Ar Lan y Mor was the place she had come in the war to have her baby and the place she had come to die and the place she had come with the Sunday school and the place she had come with father.

And she was alone with only death as her companion and not even that: death had come in and was not invited in and she was alone and she had always been alone and now her body had found a welcome relief between the clean white sheets and the smell of cabbage. And I looked at her with her white pasty lips which were no longer pink and her face which was no longer pink and her body which was no longer the body of a mother and there was something about her mouth I had always found

15

so terrifying as if one word could just finish me off, and not even a word, just a movement which would express her displeasure. Her mouth – I could never stop thinking about her mouth, and I did not truly understand why it was so terrifying.

And this was the end of my mother's life and it was the end of all her regret and all the time wasted and all the conflicts and joys and all that makes a life and there were no more tomorrows to try and make it better. She always used to say: "Tomorrow, we'll try and make it better." And I thought of Bethesda, which was my other mother: I thought of the slate grey mountains and the valley and the grey river and the oak trees, which were bare and without leaf. I thought of the grey bridges that crossed the river and the grey cloud over the dark grey slate.

My sister Janice was in charge of the body and the funeral and the money and all the administration of things, and I said it would be nice if mother could have a funeral like her mother before her in Bethesda, I said: "with a horse and a carriage." I didn't remember about the rags and the sacking just then, only the horse and the carriage: I didn't remember the face down in the earth either. It seemed right to honour my mother and the whole line of mothers, because there were so few monuments to mothers – how easily they were forgotten – and I was thinking of some means of making a distinction to say, well this was my mother.

My mother had come from Bethesda and it was the place where she was born and the place of her own mother and father, and the place where her story started and Bethesda was her place and origin and her true home. They looked at me; the sisters looked at me and they looked surprised as if I were talking from the dead. I wanted to say: "Well, I am father, I am father, I am father come home." I wanted to say: "I had to go away, and now I am come back," but they could not see me, or what I was, and I could not see me fully and what I was either.

16

Chapter Three

A walk along Coetmor New Road, my mother's funeral and a snail making its way up a freezing wall.

Catherine Alice Hughes was born in 1917 and she died in 2001 on a day I couldn't quite remember; and she was buried in Coetmor cemetery, next to Coetmor Church and she did not have her service in Jerusalem Chapel, which was in the very middle of the town of Bethesda and right close to Glanogwen Church and the old Glanogwen school house. Coetmor Church was out and it was away from the town; out of the town and mother was out and in some sad way it seemed to fit, as in life and as in death; she'd gone out of that town and the culture, which was her story, and she had married a black man. And she had her service out of the town.

The morning she was buried, bob and me and the girls walked up to Coetmor Church from Bethesda, from our home: I said it would be better to walk, and we passed the school which was my mother's last school before she went to the Home and we walked up Coetmor New Road and passed Coetmor Farm. Coetmor Farm smells and I like the smell and smelling the farm reminded me of my mother. Coetmor Hall itself was destroyed by a fire, and Coetmor Farm was all that was left. Dene Chakrabarti, who I knew quite well, said that Coetmor Church wasn't used anymore and it was the place where they put the dead bodies which were waiting to be buried and that it was the place where Dene's own baby was put when it died. She said, "That's where they put my baby when it died', and she said it in a natural way, without pity or shame. And Dene understood my mother, probably more than I did, for she was herself a mother of many children. And she was part Indian and part English.

I walked from town with bob and the girls were walking in front of us. I remember that Baba had a black woollen jacket, which she wore to school, and Yemaya had her first pair of heeled shoes and she wore a green cardigan, which was too big for her. It was a leaf green with ribs and a soft and shiny collar and her brother had bought it for her a long time after he really knew her. We walked up the High Street of Bethesda and we lived right by the Capel Jerusalem, which was Jerusalem Chapel in English and I looked up at the granite mountains behind the town and I remembered my mother saying that "Welsh people didn't need fancy architecture." She said: "Welsh people don't need fancy architecture because they have the mountains." And she would say things like that as a matter of insight and affection for the beauty of her home and it was the home of her mother, which I guess made her uneasy and troubled.

We walked up the hill by the Police Station, and 'police' in Welsh is heddlu, and along the road passed Coetmor Farm and the open fields and we walked along and we came up to the tall bare trees by the church and the old cemetery, next to the new one, and the tall trees made a gentle hissing sound. The hissing sound was made by the wind moving the few remaining dry leaves on the trees and I heard a few black birds and I saw them fly into the grey sky. I liked the sound of them.

And my mother always said that Welsh people didn't need great architecture because they already had the mountains, and what she meant was that the Welsh people already had the architecture of God; the shape of the mountains was so much more than man himself could do, and they had the valleys and the trees; for everything about her life was about God.

Coetmor Church was a small stone church surrounded by tall dark trees and some were still in dark green leaf and I saw all the people there and some were relatives and some were not. And people were wearing black and some were not. The door to the church was open and I noticed a dark yew tree beside it and I saw the old graves and I saw the grave of Idris Foster, and my mother had often talked to him and talked about him. And Idris Foster was a Welsh scholar. I saw all the people and I didn't much want to look at them or talk to them because I didn't know them any more, but Dene Chakrabarti was there because she was a friend to my mother even though she was only young. And Dene is a beautiful young woman with many children and once she came to my door when I lived in Gerlan, which is just up the hill from Bethesda.

June was there, and June had a number of children too and she had had a hard life like my mother and she was religious, but not quite like my mother and she was there with her girls: they had passed us on the road and they had waved to us. And bob and I were there with our girls.

And bob stood beside me and so did Catherine Alice, my eldest daughter who was called after my mother and I called her Baba, sometimes; and Yemaya, my youngest daughter was called after an African mother (I didn't have an African mother) and I was called Isabel after my father's mother and I was with my mother and I didn't know my father though I was him. We were standing in the freezing church right at the back and the air was biting into my skin, straight through my clothes, through my coat and through my jumper and right to my skin and my bones and every part of that church was freezing. It hadn't been warmed because it was the place where they kept the dead bodies and the service to my mother was in that place. A one bar fire was stuck high up on a wall and a red line of red heat that was not heating the room. And my mother was lying in a church where they kept the dead. I watched a snail slowly make its way up the grey stone wall by my side and I thought of a line from a poem about "a snail upon a wall, have you got at all, anything to tell, about your shell?" from a book of poetry given to me by my father, when I must have been about eight or nine. And I kept watching the snail move towards the glow of the red single bar of heat.

And it had clearly been disturbed from its sleep or its hibernation or whatever it is that snails do. And the church was full of people I did not look at and I could hear the music of Myfanwy, which was a song my mother really liked and it was a song I liked too. And it was in Welsh and I didn't know enough Welsh to know what it meant. And the words are, "Paham mae dicter, O Myfanwy, Yn llenwi'th lygaid duon di?" And in English this means, "Why is it anger, O Myfanwy, That fills your eyes so dark and clear?"

Then I saw my sister Evelyn who was two years older than me: I had not seen her for a long while and she came down the aisle and stood in front of me and said that I was to sit in the front. Her face was like she didn't know me and her hair was pulled back in the usual way and the way she wore it before the time I didn't know her, and she just said, "Go and sit in the front." And I hesitated and I said, "Is there room for bob?" and she said "No." So I thought I should obey, and I went and sat at the front where I could see where the music called Myfanwy was coming from. On the floor was a small music player and it was a shiny grey and the sound was weak and it was strained, as if it had to struggle against the freezing air. The music was weak and without heart and the sound and the warmth of the male choir voices strained against the biting cold. And I could see the coffin where my mother lay and there were colourful flowers around it.

And the names of my mother's daughters were Janice Mary, Evelyn Alice, Isabel Aileen, Charlotte Francesca and Beatrice Emma, and we all stood in a row facing the coffin and the altar according to age, but not to height and I was in the middle. And I no longer called myself Isabel Aileen but by another name. I listened intently to a young woman vicar whom I recognised from Bethesda, I think she was from Glanogwen Church; she read a piece written about my mother though she did not know my mother. She said: "She was passionate and she fought for justice," and many other things, which I do not remember. And some of the things were true and some of the things I didn't recognise to be true.

I hardly recall the hymns; perhaps one was Calon Lan, which is a well-known Welsh hymn, but I cannot remember now. And Calon Lan means pure heart or clean heart and the service was mostly in English and not Welsh, though my mother was Welsh and her religion, the one that was always not her religion, was Welsh. And I didn't know why she didn't have her service in the town at Capel Jerusalem; I wondered whether it was because her daughters were not Welsh or at least Welsh speaking, for it was a Welsh speaking chapel. I wondered about that a great deal; all the cultural incongruity of it, of black and Welsh, and of English and Welsh, and of land, and burial, and place, and where would I be buried, but I could find no answer to these riddles.

And I never did get to know why it was she had her burial service at Coetmor Church, a church that nobody used except to keep and store dead bodies as Dene Chakrabarti had said and not Capel Jerusalem which means Jerusalem Chapel and it bothered me for quite some time. But I liked the Coetmor Church for it was more of a chapel, small and plain, and had its own intimacy, and I liked the old Coetmor cemetery and I liked the Coetmor farm and the Coetmor New Road with the trees that whistled.

Catherine Alice nee Hughes was buried with her father Johnny Willy and her mother Mary and her elder sister, Margaret Louisa, in a piece of land not far from Coetmor New Road and about four or five rows from the gate and by the narrow road which leads back to Bethesda.

Several people were there though I did not look at them: I saw Verna who was a black woman and my father's sister: she looked just like him, like me, and she was posh as she always was. And she looked just like my father and I hadn't seen or remembered what my father's family were like. And I looked at the darkness of the quarry mountains, and the darkness of the valley where the town was and the houses and the Jerusalem Chapel, which was much bigger than the Coetmor Church; I saw the darkness of the other hill. Behind us was Rachub and Llanllechid and the mountains sometimes seemed to close in like huge motherly arms.

I responded to this darkness, and this is the darkness that people are apt to remember of this valley; an awesome creeping and terrible and beautiful darkness that arises and sinks; a space like the night sky with stars in it and a huge moon in it and mountains in it. And in the distance I could see St Ann's Church on the other hill and some dark trees and another graveyard and a narrow road winding upwards and I could see the dark quarry.

Chapter Four

In which there is a Great Strike and Johnny Willy has a siop, and another wife in the village.

My mother was from a town called Bethesda where there was a slate quarry, and there had been more than one in the past; and the quarry had been a place where men worked and women worked in the quarry cottages and cleaned the quarry tile floors with milk. And there were at least two quarries when my mother was a girl and one was called Penrhyn and one was called Pant Dreiniog.

Catherine Alice Hughes was born on October 17th 1917 in Bethesda and it was at the end of the Great War and fourteen years after the end of the Great Strike in Bethesda. And after the Great Strike ended, a Methodist revival came to Bethesda and it came to the Jerusalem Chapel, which is a huge and grey chapel in the town, and it is much bigger than Coetmor Church, where she had her service, and it is a Calvinistic chapel and my mother was a Calvinistic Methodist.

My mother was born above a shop called Quarry View Stores, which was in a street called Cefnfaes Street, and the land had been part of the Cefnfaes Estate and it had been built on this side of the Ogwen Valley. Her parents' shop was called Quarry View Stores because you could see the Penrhyn Quarry from the back of the house and you could see the Pant Dreiniog quarry from the front of the house. And the name of street was in English and not Welsh and the street led right into the Pant Dreiniog Quarry where the dark grey slate was mined and cut, and the grey slate had many colours and not just grey. There were huts and sheds, for cutting the slate and they were made of slate and had walls made of slate and fences made of slate and paths made of slate and pillars made of slate and in Cefnfaes Street, the houses were made of slate and the roofs were made of slate. And all the houses opposite the quarry in Grey Street and in Carneddi, all the houses which stood in rows above Cefnfaes Street were all built of slate and had slate roofs and slate fences and slate paths and little slate coal sheds and slate steps. And all those houses, some with roads and some without roads in front of them – some just with passages – were all there because of the slate. The houses were small and terraced, and some had a little square of grass at the front and some had a little square of grass at the back and there weren't many flowers in the gardens just the little patches of green. And in the gardens were little huts made of slate with grass growing on the top. There weren't many flowers in Bethesda. And above Cefnfaes Street were Bryn Teg Street and Bryn Teg Chapel; they didn't have roads in front of them and they were all built on the side of the valley alongside the quarry.

Pant Dreiniog was a great hole in the earth and it was dark and it was in the heart of the people and in the heart of the men who worked it, and a train carried the slate out of the dark hole and men gave their lives to the slate and the slate gave them a life. From the dark hole of the Pant Dreiniog Quarry the slate was sent to every corner of the globe and Bethesda was famous for its slate.

And over the other side of the valley was the Penrhyn quarry, and it was the largest slate quarry in the world and it was owned by the Pennant family who had had slave plantations in Jamaica where black people grew sugar cane and the white sugar which was untouched by human hand, which is what it used to say on a bag of sugar.

And I walked up to the Penrhyn quarry so many times; up the high street and over the bridge at Bont Twr, which means something like tower bridge in Welsh, and this is where the road meets the River Ogwen and the water just swirls about. The river itself is full of slate and some of the pieces are large and some of the pieces are small. They give the water a special colour. And I would walk over the bridge and turn left and go through the gates to the quarry, where it said beware of the dogs, and walk up to that other huge hole. And the bottom of the hole has water in it and the water looked green. The sides of the quarry are like giant steps or platforms and I heard that once there was a concert there, right down in that quarry hole during the Great Strike.

A woman called Ceinwen once told me that she remembered my mother and she remembered the old shop, Quarry View Stores and she took me home with her to Abercaseg, which is the name of the river near her home and the name of the place near the river. And she took me to meet her mother who remembered my mother. She was a very old woman and she said: "I remember the shop and I remember John William Hughes in Cefnfaes Street and I remember your mother." And on another occasion Ceinwen said: "They weren't poor like us, and they had the shop." And I didn't know them, nor did I know my grandparents. Auntie Maggie always said that the Hughes's were related to Howard Hughes in America because Johnny Willy had been born in Chicago and she went on the telly and spoke about it when he died. She said she had done her research and that she knew about Howard Hughes because he had an extra finger on his hand.

My mother was born in Bethesda and her parents' shop looked over the old Pant Dreiniog Quarry – later the quarry was filled in – and at the back it looked over the Penrhyn Quarry too. And the men who worked at the quarry walked in their heavy boots past her family shop to work and home twice every day – in the early morning and in the afternoon. They walked along the pathways in front of the houses in Bryntirion and by Grey Street. And every day there was the blasting of rock and a siren or a trumpet was always sounded first and in the very air was slate, and the quarrymen and the workers breathed it and lived it and died by it.

Her father was a shopkeeper and he sold groceries and she called him Johnny William Hughes or Johnny Willy. And in his shop he sold bacon, butter, bread, Demerara siwgr, which is sugar in Welsh and Fry's cocoa and Mellin's food. Fry's chocolate was written on the window of the shop and Rowntrees Cocoa and Rowntrees Pastilles and Carbosil and Mellin's Food and Horlicks. And the two windows of the shop were piled high with tins of beans and tins of peas and corned beef. And in an old photo I have of the shop are standing my grandmother and my grandfather and a little baby that is my mother. And there are two other people who were relations. My mother said: "That is me, the baby."

My mother said that everybody had a shop then. She said: "All the houses had little shops and some would sell hot water for a penny and some would sell soused herrings and some would sell chips." She said: "If you wanted hot water you just went with a penny to where someone had hot water yn barod," which means 'ready' in Welsh. And she said that her mother had died. She said: "My mother had died and I didn't have a mother,' and she said there was nothing for girls: "There was nothing for girls," she said.

Alongside the shop, which was called Quarry View Stores, was a rocky path which was a short cut to the town; it was a short cut to the town and it cut down steeply and it was where you had to walk carefully until you could join the other path which went on and down to the High Street where you could walk through John Street and past the old slate toilets and the slate steps. And those paths were the old paths to the Pant Dreiniog Quarry and they were well-trodden paths that the quarry men had walked up and down. And there was also a path between the houses at Pen Y Bryn and those houses were also made of slate.

My mother's father was called Johnny Willy or John William Hughes and he was a handsome man with a moustache and he must have been born about 1890 or a bit earlier and he wore a cloth cap and a suit made of wool and a waistcoat and my mother said he had another wife in the village. She said: "He had another wife in the village, and he was thrown out of the church." I don't know what happened, because my mother didn't say, and one time my Auntie Beryl, which was my mother's cousin, who had the same grandfather, began to tell me, and the story went that she, his other wife, used to live in Liverpool and then she came to Bethesda and then he, Johnny Willy, had another wife and other children in the village.

I couldn't quite grasp what that would mean in such a small town; there were so many things I didn't understand, and one of them was why the Quarry View Stores shop was gone while every other house remained in that street. Right where a shop or a building had been and where a shop had stood was an empty space. I imagined the space to be mine but at the same time I couldn't quite believe it. And the space was like not having a mother or a grandmother or a culture: the space said there was nothing there and there should have been something. And if there had been a shop or a house I could say, well this is where my grandparents lived or this is the shop, which belonged to my grandfather; but there was nothing.

And I could never understand that and I never understood how such a big shop had stood in such a small place and why when my mother's mother died, no one took those children in. I spent years wondering this and I would go up the path and look at the space hoping to find something, but there was nothing there. I asked Auntie Beryl but she didn't tell me and I thought in the end it was because of Johnny Willy and his philandering; because he had another wife in the village, and he was thrown out of the church.

Catherine Alice had four sisters, and one of them died: I heard once that the sister who died was pregnant and got pushed down the stairs but I don't know whether the story was true or not. And Maggie Louisa was the eldest and Eluned came next, and Ethel was younger than my mother, and then there was John. And when my mother's mother died all the youngest ones got sent to the Home, and my mother was brought up in a Home.

Some of the men that cut slate were called Griff and Idris and Lewis and Llewelyn and Medwyn and Rhydion, and they cut the slate, and split it into layers and drilled it and blasted it and hung from ropes and the conditions were poor. And some of the slates were huge as big slabs and some of them were small. And some of the men refused to work in the quarry, and some of them were called Islwyn and Rhys and Dafydd. And the Penrhyn Quarry was owned by a family called the Pennants who built a big castle called Penrhyn Castle, and a big bed made of slate, which weighed four tons. One man owned this entire quarry and in 1900 was the Great Strike, and the Pennant family had slave plantations in Jamaica too.

And every piece of slate was mined and carefully cut and split to the right size and each piece of slate had a man's life carved into it. And my mother looked at the men going backwards and forwards to work with their heavy boots and saw the men working and she believed that there was nothing for girls. She said to me once: "Well, there was nothing for girls." She looked out to the Quarry and she saw the darkness and she saw the oak woods and the river: she saw the great moon above Gerlan mountains and the rain which moved down the valley and swept across the mountains; she looked and she looked but she didn't see her reflection in the darkness or in the vision of the men going to the quarry and back from the quarry, and she thought, stupidly or naively, that the world belonged to men. She said to me: "There was nothing for girls," and she saw the black and white clothes and she said there was nothing for girls. She played with her sisters on the Pant Dreiniog quarry, and sometimes they took a ride on the small train carriages, which were used for the slate or they played house, but when my mother was six her mother died.

And once when I was about eight or nine my Auntie Maggie took me to the slate quarry and I watched the men splitting the slate in a huge shed and then she took me to Regent House in the town for an ice cream, and she told me about dry ice and how it was used to keep the ice cream cold. And I would never have gone to live in Bethesda if I hadn't been with Auntie Maggie, for I wouldn't have even known much about it. And later David, her son's wife, Averil, took me to see her father, and I was told to call him Uncle Glynn. I liked Uncle Glynn and he had some illness he had caught at the quarry. I remember that he lived near the place where the Purple Motor's bus, No 6, used to go and where the Purple Motor's bus no.7 used to turn and go over the narrow bridge before it turned onto the main road. Uncle Glynn lived there and he gave me a two and six piece; pressed it into my palm so I would never forget him.

And some of the men made patterns on the slate, and some men wrote their names there, and slate was used to make gates and huge high walls and fireplaces and floors. And my mother said she remembered Will Wandrin and she remembered Francon. She said: "I remember Will Wandrin and I remember Francon." And she spoke her Welsh words in English to me. She said: "And I remember going to church three times on Sunday, and to prayer meetings and to bible studies, and I knew all the words."

And I remembered Francon too, and I had seen Will Wandrin in Carneddi, a small man bent over in a dark wool coat and a cloth cap and a stick. I remembered Francon because he lived in the old slate schoolhouse at Bont Twr, which was quite close to Cae'r Berllan where I lived then with my two sons and my daughter, Baba. And 'Cae'r Berllan' was Welsh for field of orchards or something like that, and these were cottages where the families of slate workers had lived.

The cottages were quite small, and had on one side a large room all the way up to the roof, and the rest of the house was divided into two small rooms, one underneath the other. There was the cutest and steepest staircase up to the crog loft, where people slept in the roof. And the cooking was done at a stove in the huge fireplace, where there would be an open fire, an oven and a place to boil water. And when I lived there I would walk along the passage in front of the cottages until I reached the main road, and then turn right onto the bridge and round to the schoolhouse. And this was the way that the quarry men walked to the Penrhyn Quarry.

Francon had short blond hair and a straight back because he'd been in the paras. He said to me: "I remember your mother, and I remember old Johnny Willy and the siop," which is shop in Welsh, "and I was the only man in Bethesda to be in the paras." He was very handsome and he was very proud, and his face was the same kind of pink and white like my mother, and he had fair hair and he lived near me when I lived in Cae'r Berllan, and that's how I knew him, and I would meet him at the bridge called Bont Twr and I knew him because I used to walk up to the Penrhyn Quarry and he would talk to me and then he would swim in the river; and when he was done with swimming he walked proudly home.

Chapter Five

In which my mother is taken to the Home and so are Ethel and Johnny-bach.

Catherine Alice Hughes, aged six and Ethel Hughes, aged four and John Winston Hughes, aged 3, were sent to the Home at Cartref Bontnewydd, which was near Caernarvon, when their mother died. And Margaret Louisa and Eluned did not look after them, and Auntie Beryl who was my mother's cousin who had the same grandfather as my mother, did not look after them and they went to the Home at Cartref Bontnewydd, which means new bridge in Welsh and cartref means 'home' in Welsh. And Cartref Bontnewydd was a Calvinist Methodist home. And Johnny Willy let the shop go, my mother said: "He let that shop go to pieces and ruin;" and she said: "he was thrown out of the church and he had to leave his shop and he went to live in an old hut behind Number 2 bakery."

She said, my mother said, "The sins of the fathers fell on the daughters." She said it again and again to give the words more and more meaning, and this is what she said: "The sins of the fathers fell on the daughter, to the first and the second generation." I didn't know quite what she meant but I knew it came from Y Beibl, which is the bible in Welsh. And I guessed it was to do with shame and guilt and blame. And perhaps, I thought, if he had behaved to his wife she wouldn't have died, and the children wouldn't have gone to the Home and my mother wouldn't have, but it wasn't like that.

She said: "Was it worse then?" She talked like that in half completed sentences, and in a wistful and religious way as if the language itself was not hers. And she looked over the valley and the mountains of slate, and she looked at the quarry and she would remember, mostly silently. She would look at the great void and the hole in the earth's body. And my mother was a sensitive being, and when she was young she would sit on the

31

mountain grass and stare at the desolate and grey sky, she would watch the rivers explode, new, out of slate mountains, after heavy rain. And she knew that there was nothing for girls and she said to me: "I knew this then."

And the sins of the fathers fell on the daughters and the earth's first dark hole reflected nothing but was ever watchful. She said: "I felt the fear within my heart and I felt the aching loneliness, and I played house with my sisters on the quarry, but there was nothing for girls." And passion is made through hurt and through hate and through joy, and she both loved and hated her father; she hated old Johnny Willy for his absence and his lies and she said to me: "He was handsome with a long moustache." She said: "He was handsome, but he wasn't a proper dad and he got thrown out of the church because he had another wife in the village, and once he took me to Llandudno, Ar Lan Y Mor and he bought me a doll, and it broke in my hands." She said: "And the fragments fell away like childhood dreams; and they dragged me away, and I was screaming down the passage by the side of the shop and I was looking back for mother, my true mother." She spoke like that, like poetry, though she wasn't a poet. And these same words she used as a summary to her life; and she said: "Earth and blood and bones, a true testament to my sorrowed self."

My mother and her brother John and her sister Ethel were brought up in a Home and nobody else would look after them.

Once, I remember she was asked to give a talk about the Home, the Home she had been brought up in and she really wanted to but she couldn't, and she never did say much about herself. When my father went she wouldn't look for a new husband, although she still looked young and beautiful. Father was the one, it was ordained by God, and she was only having father, because he was the one. I have read that a white woman who has loved a black man can never love a white man again and I don't know why that would be. She didn't take up with anyone and she was often lonely.

It was Johnny Willy who sent them there; sent them to the Home. She said to me: "Well he couldn't manage and he let the shop go and he had so many people on his books and all of Bethesda owed him. All of his money was in the books," she said, "and he let the shop go." And she said to me: "My brother John was bad," which meant that he took the move to the Home badly and the authorities didn't let them stay together and she said: "He was screaming at the gate, they didn't let me see him, except on Sundays." She said: "I was frightened and I closed my heart to feeling and I travelled down the road of pain." And she was close to her pain, but it was of little use to her, for her pain was rarely told so that it could live and die.

And many times she would sit on the old red couch in my home in Bethesda. She had bought the couch herself many years before, second hand for a hundred pounds. And she had been so proud of it because she had never bought such a thing before: it was soft and lumpy by now and she would sit there in her darned tights and the grey shoes with laces she had worn for years, and she would be wearing the vest she had knitted and the suit she had knitted and I would bring her a hot water bottle and a small knitted blanket and I would make her some vegetable soup or lentil soup and I would hope that she would speak and sometimes she did and sometimes she didn't. Her blue glass-like eyes were full of pain and full of un-cried tears, pale blue, like water and glass. She would speak in fragments like the dry leaves thrown by the wind into the afon, which is 'river' in Welsh. And she was forgotten, and she had forgotten herself and she spoke like a bard or a preacher or something and she said: "The sacred blood flowed and marked time," and sometimes she was real and authentic and sometimes she was not.

She said: "There was already a mirror which reflected all that you were and all that you would be," and on her finger was a golden ring, which she believed in, as she believed in marriage and she believed in the one. And she was Catherine Alice

Williams and she had been Catherine Alice Hughes and she was married to Denis Williams, the famous Guyanese writer.

When they took the children to the Home, they brought a car and left it in the village and they dragged the children down the rocky path, down where the quarry men walked to and from Pant Dreiniog and they dragged them down John Street and past the old slate toilets, and past the house that had a shed at the front, and by the house with the shed at the side. Down the slate steps – they took them down the slate steps, which ran down to the High Street, just past where Lewis's the ironmongers would be. And they took them to the Home, the home that was not a home and all of her life she looked again for the home she didn't have. And she remembered always that the Home was no place for children. And she remembered the black and white clothes and she said to me: "Well I worshipped the dead god of mam," and she bore it like a sacrificial lamb.

And they made her do washing and clean toilets and learn darning and sewing and religion and ironing, which in Welsh is 'smoothio', how to be good and go to church or chapel, and Johnny-bach, her brother, was timid and dead inside and later Ethel went mad with her grief and she went funny. My mother said: "Ethel went funny and they sent her to the asylum." They sent her to Denbigh, and the day her father, Johnny Willy, was buried she wasn't there. She wasn't there, and in the newspaper it said she was otherwise engaged or some such politeness, and it said that Margaret Louisa was there and Eluned was there and Catherine Alice was there and John Winston was there, but not Ethel.

I remembered Ethel too; I remembered her in the asylum, it was 1954 or 1955 and I must have been three or four, and I looked out of the window of my father's car, which was a Rover. We had stopped at Penmaenmawr on the way, and then we were in a yard before a huge house or building, a home with many windows and it was as big as Buckingham Palace in London

34

where we lived then, and it was the place where my Auntie Ethel was, and it was just called 'Denbigh.' And even when I was quite small I knew the sadness of this place; it hung in the air, and this was the place where Ethel lived. Sometimes she was called "Mrs Barrett" and she had two daughters whom she never saw.

And I remembered Eluned, though she wasn't brought up in the Home and she was older than my mother but not as old as my Auntie Maggie; I remembered her and the leather bag she carried always and the tweed skirt she wore and the blouses she wore. I remembered her and her son Simon, who is my cousin: and she did not look after my mother, she left Bethesda and went to work for the family of the Rothschilds who had plenty of money and it was the place where she met Walter whom she married. But Maggie was not in the Home, and Eluned was not in the Home.

My mother wanted to be a teacher, and she needed forty pounds and she said to me: "I needed forty pounds to be a teacher, but I didn't have forty pounds." And it wasn't true that she didn't have anything; it wasn't true even while she believed it to be true; for passion is something, even while it is nothing, and my mother had a passion and she liked writing poems on small pieces of paper and she had a blue pen. She was articulate and she was learned, and she was literate, but all the time she believed she had nothing. And she knew what was good, and the quality of cloth and what darning to do and what outfit she could make out of nothing, or not very much. She knew all of that and she knew value, but still she thought she had nothing.

And, when I asked her, she always said: "And the sins of the fathers fell on the daughters, to the second and the third generation." And she said: "Bethesda didn't take us in," and she never could let it go, and she said: "I washed my knickers in carbolic and I read all the prayers." And she was as layers and layers of history, just like a slate mountain, and her greyness was all her colours and her greyness was her gold. And suffering was her virtue and her goodness, and she couldn't say it or speak it or transform it.

They said (to her): "Hold your tongue!" and she held her tongue and she couldn't speak and she couldn't speak of the sins of the fathers and she couldn't speak of the sins of the mothers and she couldn't speak of the sins of herself. And in my mother there was no end to deprivation, as there was no end to her hurt and there never was and there was no end to sorrow and there was no end to suffering for it was suffer little children to come unto me. And she said: "I should have been a preacher," and she fancied herself on the pulpit she did.

She had wanted to be a teacher but she didn't have the money, and when she was eighteen she left the Home and went to Liverpool to be a nurse and then she went to London to work in the Civil Service, where she met Mr Coleman and married him. And he was a soldier and she told me that she didn't like him and she said: "I was young and I was naïve and I married him and he went away to the war, and when he went to the war I met Lamar and he was a black man in the American Airforce." I was surprised and she said: "Mr. Coleman came back from the war and I had a baby and he came after me with a gun, and I was living up the Orme."

Chapter Six

In which my mother meets my father and he is a student and he is a black man.

Then she met my father, and he was called Denis and she said: "He was a young man and he was a student, an artist, and he was dirty and I taught him how to dress and wash himself." Then they lived together in Kilburn, off the Kilburn High Road in London and the Holyhead to London road runs through Bethesda, and it runs through Kilburn, and she lived in a flat about half way down the road where many of the houses were destroyed in the Blitz. Some were completely gone, and some were not and there were empty buildings and dark spaces where once had been homes and people. It was just after the war, and she had never left Bethesda even though she was living in Oxford Road in London, for she took Bethesda everywhere and Bethesda was her story. And she met my father Denis who was a young man, he was younger than she was, and she saw the quarry and the darkness of the valley in him and the passion and the enthusiasm of the people; she saw the great shadows, which are cast over the mynydd, which is 'mountain' in Welsh. Her father, Johnny Willy had said she was not to have anything to do with black men but she had darkness in her soul and the slate in her heart and the quarry and the strike and the religion and the bible and she had a dark baby. I don't know about how she met Denis, the young man who was to be my father; I don't know, except she said she met him through someone she knew and I can imagine her excitement when she saw his black face and this was the colour of the quarrymen and the dark quarry and her dark mother, who was dead, and y beibl, which was 'bible' in Welsh, and he was the colour of her shadow and the earth of her potential. I can imagine the excitement and her coming to life and her not seeing or noticing that the life of this young man was her life and everything about her life. They met and he was

37

a student and she worked in an office and she had a little brown girl and she wanted to marry someone with a dark face which was a reminder of home and she married a man with a black face, a face which was her own and she had another child. And they lived in Oxford Road, and my father was an artist. He had just finished college and he was a young black man in London and he was younger than my mother who was born in 1917 and he was born in 1923. She was older and she was Welsh and she came from Bethesda, and the pool of Bethesda was her story and she was that story.

My father was born in British Guiana and his name was Joseph Denis Ivan Williams. He was born in 1923 in Georgetown, Guyana. And my father and his family had servants so that they were not poor; as my mother was not poor until her own mother had died. They were the Williams's and they were descended from slaves who were brought from Africa from countries like Ghana and Nigeria and they were brought to Guiana in the hull of wooden ships by the Dutch and the English and the Portuguese and perhaps even the Welsh because Williams is an old Welsh name. And it is hard to imagine what being a slave might be: it means not having a name, and not having a language to speak to your family and friends, and not being able to read and having to endure terrible hardships and punishments and not having a place and being the repository for all the unhappiness of your master and all of that. And every part of your life is exploited and owned by another and you would live in slavery and you would die in it and your children would live in it and die in it. And one of the Williams's was called Moses and perhaps he was a slave and perhaps he was not, for there is not much I know about my father and his family.

The slaves were made to be English and English was the language of that oppression, and every part of the life of slaves was subject to the same violence and the same submission to the thought of the white man and the white woman and their power. And there was no way of going back to Africa or the life that was there and the relatives that were there; or the land that was there or the language that was there, or the food or the stories or the home that was there.

The white man and the white woman did everything they could to make the black man and a black woman into white people and in every possible way. And they said it was for their own good. They said: "Well, this is God's way, and it is for their own good, and we will give them a better life." So that through every generation, the Williams's were no longer Africans though they looked like Africans. They had forgotten the old life and the old ways and they became English and they were English. And each generation was English right up to when my father was born, which was just after the First World War, a war when many thousands of young men had died for King and country. And young boys in British Guiana were brought up as young Englishmen that are ready to go to war for King and country and to kill or be killed.

It's a matter of character and values and conditions and manners, and saying the right thing and all of what it takes to be a white man – manners and protocol and the literature. And his forebears were "white, of the white culture and the image of a man was white and the image of a woman was white and what was good and what you had to be was white." I've seen the old photos and the women are dressed in the long fancy dresses of the time, their dark skins against the white cloth, and the men are dressed up and they are walking amongst the white man's buildings and on the white man's roads and of course they would be going to the white man's schools and the white man's government. And they were brought up to be a white, as a white man or a white woman, and they were brought up to think that a white woman was their mother and a white man was their father even while they were black. And they were raised to make these outside images of life important.

My father, Sonny he was called as a child, or perhaps it was 'Sunny', I don't know, he was brought up in this way, which is a strange way to be brought up, but there was only the way of the white man and who could resist him? And the white man's way was the way of thought and thought was the most important way. And the white man's thought was his language. His mother's language was English and my father learnt English, and his ancestors language was English, but this was a language and a system of thought and a system of meaning which spoke against him as he was a black boy. And language is a whole complex world and not just words. It is grammar and spaces and sounds that rise and fall in certain places and it is called mother tongue, because a language is learnt from the mother. To make a language work you need other people who speak the same language, other people who understand you: a community, and in Guiana there were many communities and different groups of people. Some of those were Dutch, some were English, some were African, some were Indian and some were Chinese.

My father was from British Guiana, which meant it was ruled by the British, as Wales was, and both of them were the oldest colonies of Britain, and like Wales it was a very old colony, although I have never heard of Wales being spoken of as a colony. I didn't know him even though he was my father and even though I was him: I only knew my mother and I only knew my father through my mother and the father which was in me. He was a BG man and I knew nothing of BG because I had not been there and my father didn't talk about it, his country, like it didn't exist and he didn't talk about his father or his mother as if they didn't exist: he didn't talk about his life before he knew my mother as if it never happened. So I didn't know what he was like, and he was a stranger in my life and a dark figure in the near distance, like the dark quarry was to my mother. He was always in the distance, just like the quarry and the quarry manager, except he was a black man.

And sometimes the men that came out of the quarry were black with dust and earth and my mother knew those 'black' men from when she was a child, and her life was full of 'black' men. The first black person, a child, didn't come to Bethesda until the war came – someone told me this, and she didn't know any real black men then. Father was a real black man from British Guiana and his father was black and his grandfather was black and his mother was black and his grandmother was black. They were black all the way back to the slave ships and to Africa, even though some were light skinned and some were dark skinned and even one of the family was Chinese.

And his name was Williams, and all the way back they were Williams's and before that the family had a different name, but I don't know what that was. My father never said anything about his name and he never said hardly anything about his country or his culture. As far as I know he had three sisters and a brother, and he loved his brother who was called Everard and he was the brother that died of sickle-cell anaemia, the same brother he played with in the mud down by the river. All I know is that his parents were not poor, they had servants, and his mother was called Isabel Adonis and she liked to garden and plant flowers and she liked to make quilts. She was a lady and she lived the life of a lady, an English lady. And my father's father was a merchant and he had once prepared dinners for schoolchildren or something like that, and he had made tiles. My father told me that. He said: "He was a creative man and he was always trying different things." But he said nothing of his mother, what she was like or what she looked like or what she said or what she didn't say. He didn't say, like she wasn't there and she hadn't been there – nothing, a space, a nought, like the space in Cefnfaes Street, where my mother's parents had lived.

And Guiana was known then as 'The Garden of the Caribbean', which fed my imagination though I didn't know what it meant. The Garden of the Caribbean sounded like a nice place to be and I always loved flowers. And when father did manage to say something it sounded wonderful and exciting and romantic, and the names of the places were Demerara and Essequibo and Kaieteur Falls and Bartica and he said them all by name with affection as if they were his own. And he was brought up as an English man and he learnt to speak English as a mother tongue, and he had no other language and he knew no African language and no African name, nor did he know any African culture. Everything he might have known about Africa was gone; every story and every word and every practice was gone and he was an Englishman although his skin was black and racially he was African. He spoke English but this language didn't fit a black man though he had no other language. And the language itself embodied conflict and history and all that could be called English and much of what was known, as good English was merely a performance of words and the language made him not the person he was. And the history was in his heart, as my mother's history was in her heart.

My father spoke English, which was not a black man's language, and my mother spoke English though she was Welsh. And neither of my parents spoke a language that fit who they were, and each language was a kind of a lie to themselves. This was a problem to me, as I didn't know which language to speak. I couldn't speak my father's language because it was the language of the oppressor and I couldn't speak my mother's language – the English she spoke was not her language; that was Welsh. And I didn't know what was my language even though I could only speak English.

My father had a language to live by and perform by and know the rules of the English culture by: a house is not a pile of bricks and it wasn't just the words, the walls of the house had the job of enclosing a space, the walls had to do something and mean something and the spaces had to mean something. And his words always seemed odd to me, as an official language and these

42

words weren't his although he used them: his words were like someone who is looking outwards from a house but this house has no door and no door that opens and shuts and there is no space for people to come in and out and it was a strange language like he was borrowing it, standing at the front of a house he did not own and it was a white man's language as if he wasn't allowed in the house of the language he was standing by.

I've come back to this again and again: a house, I like to describe the language as a house – a symbolic big house of language and culture and a myriad ways of doing things and thinking about things and that language of power was a world that my mother and my father didn't and couldn't live in, and I would say: "Well this isn't his language and it isn't her language" and I would wonder what was. It affected me deeply and intimately, for language is an intimacy and sometimes I didn't know which language to speak, though of course, like him, I only knew English.

My mother was the same, although she did have a language, but it was a language she kept to herself – another house somehow which she didn't inhabit or use, or only occasionally, and it was a house which she stood at the doorway of, on the step of and didn't go in. She was Welsh, but she spoke English and she was proud that she spoke English because it gave her another culture and one with aspiration. They met in English but it wasn't their language, and they tried to make a culture, a new culture out of words and my mother was always trying to make a culture out of home, a home that had open doors and windows and my father spoke as if he had no home, save the language.

I didn't know about British Guiana; I knew only what Verna, my father's sister told me. She said that her father didn't talk to her either, except once a day, she said: "When he came home he gathered all his children together and greeted them." I think he must have been a Victorian gentleman with Victorian values that he didn't speak to his children, as my father didn't speak to us, his children. And my father had a brother who was called Everard and a sister called Eileen and another sister called Leila.

My father learnt English and he went to a school where his books were English, and the history was English and pictures were English and the poets were English men, save one woman. And it was his mother who encouraged him as mothers do, and she gave him poetry books – he liked Omar Khayyam, and she gave him paints and she made him into an English man – and how could she not? And this black woman, who was called Isabel Adonis, worked with the image of the white man and she worked with the image of the white woman to make this man who was my father.

My father told me once that he used to play in the mud and near the rivers of his home. He said: "I used to play with my brother, Everard, looking for snakes in the river and once we saw an anaconda and it was this long." He played in the mud with his brother and slate is made of mud. And I think playing in the mud is good and I think playing at the river is good and I think that being interested in nature is good.

But my father was not being raised for physical work, he was raised to be an administrator or whatever was the height of the society then, or whatever was deemed a good job then, and how could she not make him like a white man and how could she not make him in the image of a white man, because that was the only way: a society where the image of the white man is king or God. And English is the language of that God.

He was raised to work in the Civil Service and he did work in the Civil Service and then he won a scholarship, a British Council Scholarship to study in London, which is where he met my mother. And the civil service was English and British, for they were the rulers of Guiana and they called it British Guiana.

Chapter Seven

In which my mother met my father in London and she had a little
brown baby and she was brave and had honour.

And then she met my father and he was called Denis and she
said: "He was a young man and he was a student and he was an
artist and he was dirty and I taught him how to dress and wash
himself." And one of the places they lived was called Oxford
Road, off the Kilburn High Road in London. Many Irish people
lived there, and other coloured people. There were brown children in this street and all kinds of people. And our flat was about
half way down a road where many of the houses had been
destroyed in the Blitz and some were completely gone and some
were not. And my mother never left Bethesda even though she
was living in Oxford Road, in London for she took Bethesda
everywhere and Bethesda was her story, and she didn't leave it.

Her father, Johnny Willy had said she was not to have anything to do with black men but she had darkness in her soul and
she had a dark baby and she defied him as he had abandoned her.
I don't know about how she met Denis, the young man who was
to be my father; I don't know.

She worked in an office and she had a little brown girl and she
wanted to marry someone with a dark face which was a reminder
of home and she married a man with a black face, a face which
was her own and she had another child, which was my sister
Evelyn. And they lived in a flat in Oxford Road, and my father
was an artist and he had just finished college and he was a young
black man, younger than my mother who was born in 1917, and
he was born in 1923. She was older and she was Welsh and she
came from Bethesda and the pool of Bethesda was her story and
she was that story.

I remember Oxford Road because it was my first home and it
was the home of my mother and my father and my sisters and
their names were Janice Mary, and Evelyn Alice, and Charlotte

Francesca, and there were trees on either side of the road which made shadows over the pavements, and some of the houses had been bombed and some had not. The houses which had been bombed were at the top of the road and they were completely black inside and out. And I was interested in this blackness and it intrigued me and next to the house where we lived was a space, like the one in Bethesda, though I hadn't been in Bethesda then. It was a space where houses had been and people had lived. And the children of the street played in this space and some of them were called Alexander Baron and the 'Roughsedges', who were Irish, and even at a young age I thought that was the right name for rough boys. And I remember one of these boys cut my face with a knife.

And we lived in the middle of the road in a Victorian house, which was divided into flats. We lived in the middle of the road and in the middle flat. Mr Kerman lived in the basement and I was frightened of him because he was old and he had a wife and I had heard that rats lived in basements. And he wore a mackintosh which wasn't quite grey and wasn't quite brown. I think it is an English colour to fit into the English way of living and he wore a cloth cap made of tweed. His wife wore a mackintosh and she had a shopping bag over her arm and her hair was rolled at the front with rollers and she often had a headscarf on her head.

My mother's hair was not like that: I don't think she wore hair rollers and I don't think she wore a scarf tied at the top of her head with the rollers sticking out the front. Her hair was lovely and kind of fluffy and the light shone through it.

I do not know who lived in the ground floor flat or who lived in the top flat and to get to our flat you had to walk up a tall staircase, which was painted in a brown sticky paint. Around 1955 or 1956 the people in the ground floor flat had a television and they watched Robin Hood and they watched Muffin the Mule, and when I looked through the keyhole I could see their little brown telly.

A narrow piece of stair carpet was placed in the middle of each stair and it was held down with stair rods. And when you climbed the stairs it was our flat, and my mother and my father and my two sisters lived in two large rooms and a small kitchen and bathroom. And my mother was pregnant; I think it was one of my first memories and she went to hospital to have a third daughter, who was called Charlotte Francesca.

And many years later, when she was living in Bangor she told me that when she was pregnant with me my father told her to have an abortion and he didn't want another daughter, and she went to Harley Street to see a doctor, and not Dr Wistrich, the Polish doctor who was over the road from our flat. She went to Harley Street and paid to see a doctor and he said: "There is no abortion unless you are a mad woman," and there were no abortions then, only back street ones and my father took my mother to another Home so she could get an abortion, but she didn't have one. She said: "He came to fetch me because he couldn't manage without me; your father couldn't cook an egg."

So I was born in 1951 and I was named Isabel, a name that made me different to my sisters, as I was named after a black woman and not a white woman. And my mother made me different and I was different. And whatever plans my mother and my father had for me, I survived them and from that time I was different and set apart. And I don't think she made me different deliberately, she did it unconsciously to give expression to herself or some part of herself that I might be – or maybe it was him.

In the front room of our flat was the sitting room, and it was also a bedroom for my parents and a studio for my father. His books and his Sobell radio were there. And everything, the whole world, was my father's and not my mother's, because she didn't believe in it and nothing was hers and no wanting was hers. A fire burnt in the hearth on cold days and she would bring the coal up from the basement yard in a bucket, and I would sit by the window and wait for father to come home.

My father went out to work and sometimes my mother went out to work. I think he was a teacher of some kind; an art teacher, perhaps, and there was an excitement about him, as there is with men: a kind of sexual excitement, as if they have the life and a woman hasn't. Father went out to work and he came back, and my mother cooked for everybody and did shopping for everybody and washed clothes for everybody. She would take me to school and the school I went to was called St. John's. Sometimes she would take me down to the bottom of Oxford Road to a little shop and she would buy things with her coupons, since it was just after the war. I would sit on a chair by the counter and wait for her and watch her take out her coupons and give them to the shop lady. And in that street was the sugar lump man, who had a little brown tin with writing on and it was full of sugar lumps, lined up in neat rows and which he gave to the children in the street.

And in the kitchen of the flat I remember the huge tins of National Dried Milk – they were white tins with a blue band on the top and blue writing on and my mother mixed the powder and made cocoa and semolina and custard with this dried milk. There was a scoop to measure out the dried milk and I liked to put the powder in my mouth and feel it go all pasty. And sometimes she bought Carnation milk, and I liked to drink that too. She opened the tin with a thing that made a triangle opening so that I could drink the sweet milk. She let me have all kinds of food, puddings and such, because when it was meal times I could not eat. I was hungry and I drank evaporated milk from the larder and I could not eat at the table.

I watched her do the washing: she put the wet clothes through a mangle in the back garden. And the washing was hung up on a pulley at the back of the house. And all the houses had pulleys and washing at the back of the houses which were mostly flats. And Monday was the washing day. We were poor and she saved rags and glass jars and bottles and everything she could for the rag and bone man. He would come into the street and cry: "Rags and bones, rag and bones", in a strange high pitched voice, and then she would collect a sixpence, or a shilling from him and that made her happy. And sometimes he had goldfish in jam jars. I liked the rag and bone man because he had interesting things. We were poor and many of the people in the street were poor and my mother remained poor until she died, even though by then she had a little money.

My father painted in the front room and there was a painting of my mother there and it said, Catherine Alice, 1951 on it and it was painted on a piece of board, which was long and rectangular. The painting was kind of blue, and in the picture she looked all stiff, and her hair looked like she had had it in rollers. She always did that; just made her body all stiff like a soldier when someone was looking.

In the corner of that small front room was another painting of lines and colours, and my father was a painter. Sometimes he took us to see Ben Enwonwu who was the Nigerian artist who made a sculpture of the queen. He had a small son and I remember the son, in a high chair, a son that kept throwing food on the floor. And Ben Enwonwu was the first black man to make a sculpture of the queen, although I don't think people spoke in that way then, as if life was some endless competition for who was first, a white man or a black man. We didn't live in a world of numbers back then.

He would take us there and to see other artists, and artists would come to our home. Some of them were Wilson Harris and Cy Grant and Jan Carew and they were men that were to become famous. And I heard that father shared a studio with Francis Bacon near the railway lines, but I don't know if that was true, and my mother said she had met Mervyn Peake, and that he smoked more than one cigarette at a time and that he had been to the concentration camps; but I don't know if that was true either.

My mother wasn't an artist or a painter, but she was always creative and making do and sometimes she would sketch a little and she drew a picture of geraniums and she liked to draw flowers and she would collect the paper from flour sacks and waste brown paper and open it carefully and stick it on the wall in the kitchen, so that her daughters could draw on the wall, and all her art was not called art, but all her making things and making do were her art. And sometimes she had to go out to work and sometimes she didn't; we were very poor, and we went to nursery, and to an after school club where there was bread and dripping to eat and white bread with just the vaguest hint of jam. And sometimes there were games and I didn't like them. And when the after school club was over, my sister and I had to walk home past the bombed buildings.

Occasionally at weekends we would go to Bromley to see my mother's friend, Lynette, who was Welsh. Lynette was a Welsh woman from South America; she was a writer and a poet and a painter and she had been at the same college as my father. My mother would take us to Waterloo station, me and my sisters, who were called Janice and Evelyn, and my sisters would be dressed in gabardines or woollen coats, with hair neatly oiled and plaited, with shoes polished and shining. Whatever it was we were wearing had been lovingly washed and mangled and aired and ironed and love put in, for this is or was women's work and it was the world of my mother. And we would get the train to Bromley and leave the city and see the countryside.

My mother named my sisters Evelyn and Beatrice after Lynette, because those were her other names. And Lynette had a gypsy caravan, and she had creative ideas and she had an idea to make an underground gallery at Chislehurst Caves. My father began to paint there with another young man, a sculptor called Peter Danziger and one day the roof of the cave fell in. And Lynette was interested in the Druids and the old religion and The White Goddess and she helped Robert Graves to write, and the caves were a place where Druids had been.

And I know all about this from Lynette's daughter who is called Angharad and Lynette's son who is called Prydein and one time we went back to the caves to find the painting: and my father's painting was still there, and it had been there in the dark for fifty years and only seen by the visitors to the caves.

And when I was in the station at Euston and I was putting on my make-up Angharad said to me: "I remember your mother in Oxford Road; she was dressed all in colours and she wore a big skirt, and she wore lipstick like you." And in some strange way, Angharad looked like my mother: her hair was like my mother's had been. And Angharad had found a photo, which is the reason we got together and in the photo was a young black man with a baseball cap, and in front of him are small paraffin lamps and he is painting a cave. And the man is my father.

Chapter Eight

In which Auntie Maggie was my mother's eldest sister and she came to our flat in Oxford Road with tins of sweets and she and my mother would speak in Welsh.

My mother spoke Welsh to Auntie and they would open their separate house of the Welsh language – for languages bring people together and they pull them apart. And they would open the doors and they would open the windows all the way upstairs and into the rooms. And some people speak and they make their words a mystery: a lot of people do this and believe this. And when I hear people speak Welsh to each other I am amazed how the language changes and how different it is and how it is full of emotion and not at all like English. English is a very different kind of language and it is a language, which has been used to dominate, and it is a language that has been used to subjugate and it is a language for the novel and there is much that is strange about it.

Auntie Maggie and my mother spoke Welsh. And I did not speak Welsh, though it is my mother's tongue, and I learnt to listen to Welsh without knowing it and I learnt the different sounds and I stood outside the house while I stood inside of it. And my mother had not taught me to speak Welsh. Auntie Maggie was my mother's older sister and she had gone into service and she hadn't looked after my mother. She worked in London and she had persuaded my mother to come to London where she met father.

And whenever I think of Auntie Maggie I always think of home because she had married Uncle Matt who was a builder, and he had built her a bungalow in Penrhyn Bay in Wales. What Auntie Maggie really wanted was for us all to go and live in Wales, for wherever my mother was, she wanted to be close by, because she needed my mother. But my mother was married to a black man, so that made things different and my father couldn't live in Wales.

I looked forward to her visits because she was always smiling and she always had sweets, which were in short supply in our lives. Sometimes my father would stop his car and buy Sharps toffees, and he would buy Peter's chocolate for himself, which are little discs of dark chocolate wrapped in foil but that was all. And if I wanted something sweet I would mix up cocoa and sugar and put it in a small piece of greaseproof paper and eat it in the night when my mother was not looking. Somehow I learnt early on that the enjoyment of food must be hidden.

Auntie Maggie had sweets and they were real sweets, which came in round tins with pictures of beautiful white Victorian women in quite wonderful clothes, and the sweets were in coloured wrappers and the colours were gold and green and purple. Sometimes my mother made home made sweets which weren't at all like Auntie's, and she made them taste of mint and white paste and she made the strangest truffles with dusted cocoa powder.

The way they spoke was strange, and the two of them, my aunt and my mother, were locked into this strange talk: she spoke to my mother in Welsh and then she spoke in English and then she spoke again in Welsh in her high pitched voice. She said: "Lull, lull," and she was always talking religion and talking chapel and how she'd seen Him at the back door and she said: "I saw Him at the back door," and: "When I went for the coal, He was there." And she was talking about Jesus and she was waiting for the Resurrection and the hand of God on her.

I don't think she was wearing the cross then, the cross that she would wear later to show that she was the anointed one, and one of the special ones which God had chosen. I think she thought that my mother wasn't one because she had married a black man. And she spoke of spirits and the after-life and she spoke of visions, and when my parents brought me my first doll at a jumble sale, I was sure it was alive. Then I was scared of dolls.

And in those days my father had to have a car as there is

nothing like a car to show that you are successful, and it was a symbol of his success in the white man's world and one day he said: "Rover," and there was a Rover car in the street outside our flat. That car was elegant and it had two big lights at the front and a fog lamp, and down the sides it had running boards. I used to watch him cranking it through the window.

I was only a toddler; I looked out of the window and I watched him crank up the car and it wasn't just Auntie Maggie who was the anointed one. We didn't have any money, but father had to have a car because his enjoyment was worn outside and not in stealth, and it was big and black with leather seats and running boards on either side. God and mammon stood side by side: Auntie Maggie wanted us to go and live in Wales, and now we could go there on our holidays.

My mother would wake us in the night, and my father would drive us through tree filled roads, all the night until we got to Wales. And then we would stay at Auntie Maggie's new house in Penrhyn Bay. I loved the country, but when I saw the country near the sea I loved that too. And the first time we stayed at a huge red bricked house on the sea front at Rhos on Sea, near the little church and Auntie Maggie said she had seen my father's mother, though she was already dead, and whose name was Isabel Adonis, and she said: "I saw Denis's mother by Batty's, and she said she wanted him to go home to Guiana." And that was the way she talked and I don't know if it was true or not. And that holiday I saw ghosts in the red-bricked house.

And the next time in Wales it was to stay at Batty's in Penrhyn Bay: we stayed in a caravan and there was just the one caravan in the field, a field that was part of a farm with many black and white cows. I think it might have been called Batty's field or Batty's farm, or something like that. My mother said that I was ill and she said: "This girl is ill," and she looked after me once, and she looked after me twice, because she had to put twice into everything. And we stayed in the caravan and she washed our clothes in a tin bucket, and she washed me in a tin bucket and she washed my sisters in a tin bucket. And there was a dairy and it was full of black and white cows and I always thought that the smell of cows was the best smell ever.

And Batty's was an old monastery and the peace of the monks was still there, residing within the trees or the air and the rustling of the trees. You had to go up a narrow lane to the field and at the top of the lane was a gate, and father said for us to open the gate. He said: "If you are good, I will let you stand on the running board, or I will let you sit on the bonnet of the car and you can open the gate."

Auntie Maggie's house was the first home I knew that seemed like a home should, and it was the nearest place to a home. You had to go along Llandudno Road, just by the toll bar and go in the side door to the kitchen. You had to walk up a steep path, which was paved in a crazy-paving kind of way, and approach the side door. And not the front door: you weren't to use the front door, and the back entrance led into the kitchen and behind the kitchen door was a walk in larder which was full of food, and I had never seen a cupboard with food in like that. And amongst the tins of food was Koo jam from South Africa and tins of salmon, and tins of evaporated milk and special cheese and Welsh butter and tins of Spam and triangular tins of ham and the butter was wrapped in greaseproof paper, and there was white bread with white flour on the top, and cakes called custards from Sumners in Llandudno. This was nothing like my mother's cupboard and it was like a siop or a store or something. And her kitchen table was piled up with things, like old copies of newspapers and piles of ironed napkins and she had that blue and white crockery and a box, which was full of Cox's apples, and she had wrapped each one in old bread paper.

She had ham on the bone and Auntie Maggie was rich, at least comfortable and in every room were boxes filled with bargains and some of these were shoes, and hats and coats, and more cutlery, so very shiny and probably unused, and more cups and all of it was new and it was for the Lord. Her carpets were clean: they were deep and warm, and not at all worn, her wood floors were polished with Mansion polish and it smelt that way and she kept white sheets on the parlour chairs so they wouldn't get messy. And there was plastic on the floor because Uncle Matt was a builder, though I don't remember Uncle Matt's chair being covered. She had a son called David who liked cycling and on the photo in the front room it said David Rutherford, champion cyclist, or something like that. And in the front room was a round table, which was the table of the Lord.

And Auntie Maggie always said that she had made some scones, and she said: "I've made you some scones and they're as big as this," and she would hold up her index finger and use it as a measure with her other index finger on her other hand and the scones were always cooked in a very hot oven so that they shot up as peaks. They weren't scones at all, I learnt later, they were small sponge cakes. And she always got her words mixed up like my mother, and it was amusing to listen to her. She stoked her stove and talked incessantly about the bargains she bought at Woods's, Colwyn Bay, and sometimes she cooked bara brith, which is 'fruit bread' in Welsh. She had the recipe for bara brith on an old piece of paper, which mentioned how to use your old tea to soak the fruit. And everything in her kitchen was new and clean, and her furniture in her house was from Rhydwen, Jones and Davies.

And Auntie Maggie had no problem with desire because it was all for the Lord, or it was all for father, but it was not for her, and she had stainless steel worktops and an electric toaster, and she had central heating, and a huge telly with a sliding door, so she and father could watch the Black and White Minstrels. I hadn't connected them, the Minstrels, with my father or black people and they were of no interest to me, and I had no awareness of race or blackness, and if I had it was a shame buried deep within me.

Chapter Nine

In which I am being pushed up Oxford Road in a pushchair and passing the bombed buildings and looking at my little hands and there are no nails in them, and my father paints.

I look at them and I notice that my nails are not there and they have fallen out. And in another memory I have fallen out of the pram – a high pram, and my chin is all cut and my mother has to take me to hospital and they sew the pieces of flesh together. Then I begin to have a mysterious rash on my body, all over my legs and my face. My mother takes me to see Dr Wistrich across the road, who was a Polish Jew. He said to her: "This is ring-worm", and she said to me: "This is ringworm," like a death sentence, as it was to her something terrible and irrevocable. And she had a way of saying things, like: "Hell and damnation," like: "Every human flaw is a sign of the devil," and the most impor-tant thing was to be clean, because being clean was a sign of virtue. And she was always cleaning and scrubbing and slopping water about.

So Dr Wistrich gave my mother a black cream for my rash in a huge brown pot and she bathed me and my poorly legs in Wright's coal tar soap, which was the best for my condition. And when I was about four or five I was tested for TB because one of my mother's friends had had TB; and then I had worms and had to hide in the toilet and fill jam pots with the worms. The bathroom in the flat had a huge gas boiler on the wall; it was terrifying to see the flames and to see my mother light it. She would have to lean over the bath and light it with a rolled up and lighted taper made from twisted newspaper. She was always saving hot water and making the children bathe in the same water, and she washed us with red carbolic soap, our hair and everything, to make us clean.

I always seemed to be ill; I seemed to live on the edge of my mother's life, and I was on the edge and at the same time right in the middle, like she really needed me, and I was both deprived and spoilt. My mother had to be two mothers at once because she hadn't had a mother: she was the mother she was, and the mother she was always trying to be. She said: "Isabel, you will never be able to do anything, you'll never be able to drive a car, you'll never be able to have a job," and she believed it, and I believed it. And mostly she was talking to herself and not to me. And she was always trying not just to look after me, but look after me better, and that meant making me good and clean.

When it came to looking after me she was over protective and over caring and she was so busy making me different and special and she said: "She is sensitive," and then my father said: "There is something wrong with that girl," and my mother told Verna, my father's sister, to keep me away from my other sisters, and she told Gordon and Sheila to keep me away from my mother and my sisters. I went on the bus to Kensington with my Auntie Pinxie – her name was Verna – and I went to Holland Park with Gordon and Sheila, and my parents were always trying hard to keep me separate and different. But there was nothing wrong with me except the way she made me, and the more she kept me away from her the more I needed and wanted her. And she made me like herself: almost like an orphan. She put me out, so I could be like her; and she put me out like her family had put her out and the past ruled and was never changed.

Me and my Auntie Pinxie were very close and we went to Kensington on the red double-decker bus together. She was quite the poshest person I had ever seen and all of her clothes were carefully chosen and some of them were home made. I heard once from someone else that she was voted the most attractive and most well dressed person in Guyana which was the old British Guiana and she certainly always looked like that. She was a high up secretary and had worked for all kinds of posh people, like banks and she was very posh. And she looked just like my father and had the same mouth with a slightly overhanging lip and she had eyes just like him; a bit slanting, on account of the Chinese blood or genes in her and she had that same rich brown colour which was quite different from my skin colour. And all my life I went to see her: I found her in different places in London and sometimes it was a small bed-sit flat and sometimes it was a big flat; I always kept in touch because my father was gone and she was the only black family I knew. She looked after me, but part of her looking after me was to keep me away from my family and who is to know if that was a good thing or not.

And it was only me that kept in touch with her. I asked her why my parents had sent me out and she said: "They sent you out because you were very sensitive," and she never said anything else. She wouldn't have any talk of race and she wouldn't have any talk of colour or anything like that, but it was because of her that I found out the things I did about my father and his family.

Well my mother was lovely, and she looked lovely, and her hair was golden brown and a little bit red: she would wear strange colourful skirts and little jackets and rose pink lipstick. Her skin was what is called white, though it was not the colour of white paste. And she always made out that she loved me the most, and she was always saying throughout my life: "I loved you the most, more than the other girls," and then she started saying things like: "Oh, Isabel you have a different brain," and things like that. I don't think she knew that she was doing it; I do not think so at all.

My father won a painting competition and he did lots of painting in the front room, which was up the stairs from the front door and he met lots of important people and one of them was called Wyndham Lewis who had written a book saying what a good man Hitler was. He was a white person and my father needed white people, but he didn't want to need white people. And this is a matter of fact, that in the end there was always the white man, who he wanted to get away from. My father said he was going to Africa to escape from the white man, he said: "I'm going to Africa, to Khartoum and I'm going on a plane and you will come afterwards on a boat." So father went off to find the Dark Continent, which is called Africa. And he began to search for himself, the black man, which was the person he already was.

The white man was always right there inside him, and the white man was there outside him, and the white man was everywhere and there was no escape. So my mother made our hair like white girls, and it was brushed and brushed and 'coomped', she called it, getting the knots out with a Mason Pearson brush, and plaited and groomed. And my mother hated my hair, and she said that I should go to my father, and she said with exasperation: "Go to your father and he will do your hair." And my father brushed my hair and pulled it and groomed it and plaited it so that it was a punishment and without joy. And it was a punishment to have frizzy hair.

So my father went to the Sudan to look for himself; the self he was already. And when he left London he was a painter. He had been working at the Central School of Art as a teacher and he was a visiting tutor at the Slade School of Art, and he was doing well and he was painting, and this painting was his blackness and this painting was his mother. And every man is looking for his mother and every man is looking to leave his mother, and when he went to Africa he was looking for his mother, the one he was trying to leave. He was successful and he had been runner up in a competition which was called the Daily Express Young Artist's Exhibition, but that didn't satisfy, and his desire to be famous or recognised didn't satisfy, and it was not experienced or complete. He had success and he didn't have success, and success is supposed to make him feel good but it makes him feel bad. As it was with my mother: her desire was always a not-desire, as if desire was something she couldn't have even as she had it.

We moved to Africa, and it was 1957 or somewhere around

that time and I can't quite remember. I was six years old or nearly six; I had been in the first class at St John's School in Kilburn and I had been in Mrs. Angel's class and I don't recall if I went to Mr Rawbottom's or Mr Robottom's, or some such name. My father left and my mother stayed behind and then we went on a long trip to Liverpool; and we had a trunk and new dresses and coolie hats, because my mother's friends Gordon and Sheila had taken us up the West End to buy all the things we needed. I had a blue and white sailor's dress and my sister had dresses with spots on. I had always wanted a pair of shorts and they bought me red shorts with white stitching on.

And Gordon was a Jew and he had escaped from Hungary and my mother always said, "Jew" or "Jew boy" in such a strange way, like there was a funny taste in her mouth, as if she was ashamed, as if she were expressing her very voice of shame. And that self-same shame was laced with her disgust of herself, and her disgust about money, and her disgust about intimacy and desire, and her disgust with food, and her disgust about talking, and it all came out of her open lips and in those few words, "Jew and Jew Boy." I have often thought about this and what happened to the Jews and no other word she spoke said so much about her sense of alienation.

Chapter Ten

In which a little girl plays in the white sun and goes to live in a bigger house where there are black servants.

I am a little girl with short thick plaits and ribbons, and I played hopscotch on the veranda on the balcony of the Red Sea Hotel. The sun is fierce and hot but it doesn't bother me too much. The ground beneath my feet is beautifully tiled in rich blues and reds, squares that are bound by black lines, and I am using the shapes to hop and jump between them. My sister and I played hopscotch in London, in Oxford Road, but we are in Africa now. I look up at the sun and I have my coolie hat on, and I have a sailor's dress, which is a deep blue with a large white collar, and I have on white Clark's sandals, which have holes at the front.

We have come through the Suez Canal which was man-made I am told, though I don't know what man-made is. And the boat moved slowly down the canal, and sometimes you could see ancient Egyptian temples made of sandstone, but I don't remember seeing pyramids, and the boat moved slowly. I remember people on the boat talking and they were talking about the 'Suez Crisis' and how our boat was the first boat through. They said: "This is the first boat through the Suez," and all around us we could see the yellow sand and the temples. I liked the boat, but not when it went through the Bay of Biscay. I would sit on the deck, and the steward would bring some beef tea in small white bowls, and he was carrying a tray full of these white bowls. He had a way of walking that made him look like he was walking sideways, like an acrobat with many small white bowls balanced before him.

My mother would say: "Drink your beef tea," and she would go off and leave me sitting with a blanket on a chair on the deck with the heaving blue sea before me, and when I felt better I played quoits and wandered about the ship; and I always felt a sense of loneliness ever since I can remember. The food on the boat was so different from Oxford Road.

My mother is asleep and my sisters are asleep and I am playing in the hot sun.

The shoes are white, with a T bar and air holes to keep the feet cool. My mother cleans them for me with chalky white polish and she rubs hard over the dark scuffs. On my head I am wearing a Chinese coolie hat to protect me against the hot tropical sun. Inside the hotel my mother is asleep and so are my sisters. My father is in Khartoum and he has sent an agent to help my mother. She says: "The agent has come to look after us." I don't like the agent and he is slimy and greasy, and he's tall with a little book and a short pencil, which he puts in his mouth every now and then to wet it before he writes in his book.

He is tall and his hair is greased back, and he wears a European jacket and trousers though he's not an Englishman. My father has sent him to help my mother in this new country with her four children. I don't trust him, and he's helping my mother with her shopping and buying her cigarettes and running errands for her, but all the time he's writing notes with his wetted pencil, which he moistens with his mouth. He makes as if to help her, but he is only helping himself and I'm frightened of him and I'm keeping out of his way.

He has a cigarette lighter shaped like a gun, and he is very anxious and at the same time humble when my mother pulls out her silver cigarette case and removes a cigarette. She likes being posh and she's got a cigarette holder too and when she smokes a cigarette she looks funny, like she's playing at being posh. He pulls the trigger, and I'm terrified; a flame pops out of the top of the gun. He thinks it's funny, but I don't.

The hotel is elegant and built by the British, and it has several rooms, and the floors are as huge as spreading quilts, and I play hopscotch and I do not touch the lines, for my sister says that to touch the lines is dangerous. She says: "If you walk on the lines then your mother is a swine."

Some of the floor is burning hot and some of it is cool, and I walk through over the cool tiles, and go downstairs into the foyer, where there is a small shop run by a Lebanese man. On the shelves are rows and rows of dolls, which fascinate and frighten me. I remember my wind up yellow tractor with its large key which my mother has left at home in London, a home that isn't a home any more, and the shop man begins to wind up the dolls, and he says I can sit on his knee. Then he starts to kiss my ear and he puts his hot tongue in my ear, and I run away and return to my mother. He kisses my ear with his spit and I run away to see my mother.

We sleep in the Red Sea Hotel and we eat in the Red Sea Hotel: we go down to the dining room which is dark and cool, and the waiters have long white shirts and we are waited on by them. And then we are all posh and we sit down with my mother, and we are dressed up and clean, and our hair is all plaited and pulled and oiled. She puts olive oil on our hair: it's one of those things like Welsh butter and Dettol, the things she believes in. We sit down and we behave and my mother says: "Behave yourself, because you are ambassadors," or something like that. And my mother is caught between going up in the world and being down in the world.

The waiters come by our table and their skins are darker than our skins; they have long white shirts and behind them the room is dark with small spaces of light. They have heavily pressed damask cloths folded neatly over their dark arms up to their dark fingers, and they have little cotton hats on their heads and they move silently amongst us as if we were in church. It is a kind of church where white people rule, and we eat egg and bacon and sausages and we are very posh, if only for a while, and we are going up in the world. The atmosphere in the darkened room is quiet, gracious – and I am quiet too and well behaved as a princess in my new dress and my oiled and plaited hair and my white shoes.

My mother reminds me constantly how to eat with all the different cutlery, and how to drizzle soup gently into my mouth without opening my mouth wide, and she's keen on etiquette and she says: "You lift the spoon so that it's flat, and you move it towards your mouth like this," and she lifts up her spoon without dropping any soup whatsoever. And I look across at her as she instructs me. This is followed by instructions on how to eat fish with a knife and fork, and how to recognise a steak knife – it has a serrated edge – and how to eat bread rolls correctly. She said: "You break off a small piece in your hand, and you take a little patted butter, and you gently put it on the bread." And she would say: "You don't open your mouth wide and you put a small piece of bread in and you chew slowly and you close your mouth." And she tells me that when you want to pick up a bone and want to use your hands you must ask to bone. She said: " You must say, 'May I bone?' before picking up a lamb chop." And the rules of eating were tedious and endless, and even back in our little flat I could scarcely eat, and she was always trying to make me, but now I must watch my p's and q's and sit in silent moments in the darkened room watching the light on the bright blue sea.

And my mother eventually has a row with the Egyptian agent when he takes out his notebook and his wet pencil and delivers her a huge bill: I don't know if she pays him or not but she is furious and we depart from the portals of luxury for our next journey which is the long train journey between Port Sudan and Khartoum.

In our little flat in London there was no space; in Africa space is without end, and it awakens something deep inside me where God lives all the while. It's nothing at all like London, even though the British have been doing their best to make the whole world like them. My mother has put together a stock of tin cans for the trip on the train, which will take two days. She has rice pudding, Carnation milk and sardines in olive oil and a bag full of African bread rolls, which are sour and yeasty. My mother really likes sardines but not in tomato sauce. She likes to open them up and remove the backbone from each fish, and then eat them with toast. She has a small silver pocket knife, which she uses to cut the bread, and we picnic on these frugal but tasty rations.

The journey on the train is slow: if I look out of the window I can see the back of it winding slowly through the red desert like a giant caterpillar. It's such a strange sight because of its relation to the endless emptiness, just the train and its shadow and the desert. The train, like the hotel we've left behind has the same decaying splendour, a remnant of British rule, with polished mahogany and brass fittings in each compartment. Beds are suspended from the ceiling and a small sink falls down neatly from the wall where my mother washes our bowls and spoons, and we are going to Khartoum to join my father, and I am fascinated by this miniature world where I can pretend to be posh and refined.

During the night an inspector boards the train to check our passports, waking us all from sleep: my mother has a row with him, which is something to do with certificates and the right injections. My mother always has to fight about everything; she's a white woman travelling alone with four black children and her anger makes her real and terrifying; I am frightened of her and other people are frightened of her. She's unpredictable and her anger sits there to protect us, like an animal waiting for some reason to be released, and she always battles her way through officialdom and she sees off the night intruder.

And stretched between the long nights are two long suffocating days. And I wander up and down the train listlessly amusing myself by making fun of the other passengers, and staring out of the window and watching the occasional mounted baying donkey making its lonely way across the sand.

As the train draws into Khartoum my father is waiting at the side of the railway track in the dark and he steps out of the dark in a suit made of khaki, which he has had handmade by a tailor, I don't recall the station, just a stop and a man stepping out of the darkness and the man is my father. He takes us to the Mogram, which is an area of Khartoum and that is what it is called. And this is where we are going to live right in front of the KTI where my father has his new job.

After the two rooms in our London flat, our new home is huge: it's long, with a flat roof and it stands in its own compound, which consists of a large expanse of grass. At the front is a large gate and on the other side of the road is the college where father goes to work.

The servants' quarters are at one side of the house, and at the other is the main entrance, which leads into a large living room where the chairs are arranged in a square. There is no fireplace and the place is dark or at least kept that way, since the shutters are kept shut. In the corner of the room is a door, which opens out onto a sizeable veranda and the garden at the back of the house. And there are no flowers in this tropical garden just a huge expanse of grass that doesn't look like English grass, and in the trees are large black birds. From the veranda are steps leading up to another open space, directly above it where my parents sit in the evening drinking sweet tea made with evaporated milk and lumps of sugar in the orange light of dusk. My mother always forbids us to jump from the steps or the roof and she says that we will hurt our wombs. To be a woman is pain and suffering we must endure. To be a woman is to suffer.

Chapter Eleven
In which there are no flowers in the African garden and in which there is only one and no other.

Catherine Alice Hughes was born in Bethesda in October 1917, and Bethesda is in Wales and the people there speak Welsh: and she was orphaned at an early age and she was brought up in a Home and she didn't have a mother. And her father who was called Johnny Willy was a grocer and he had two wives in the village and when his wife died he went to pieces and he lived in a hut made of slate behind No. 2 Bakery and not No.1. And she went to London and married a man she did not love and then had a baby with a man she did love, but he went back to America. Then she met another man who was a black man and they lived in London and then they went to Africa and they lived in the Mogram.

The Mogram house was long and of a rectangular shape; behind it was a road into the town, and on one side of the road, near to the house was a large prison made of mud. The tall walls were made of mud and it glowed red in the evening sun. The road led into Khartoum, which had a large market, and in the market people sold paraffin for cooking, and all kinds of spices and fruits and vegetables, and huge blocks of halva, which looked like cheese. There were tall colonial buildings and a palace by a river, and the river was called The Nile. And we didn't live far from the Nile or the palace and by the side of the Nile we could see the bridge that went to Khartoum north and we could see the bridge that went to Omdurman, where there was the Blue Nile and the White Nile. And sometimes my mother and my father went to parties at the palace, and my mother once told me that she had met Haile Salassie, but I didn't know where and I didn't care.

The river was lovely and the walk by the river was lined with neem trees, and a great moon hung there sometimes. On the river were all kinds of boats, and my favourite were the paddle steamers. And over the river were open land and goats, and men with donkeys, and women walking in indigo clothes, and the smells of Africa and the sounds of singing and drums.

At one end of the Mogram house were the servants' quarters – we had two servants – and at the other was a door to the main house into the living room, where the chairs were arranged in a square. There was no fireplace and the room was dark, or at least it was kept dark with the shutters closed, and in the corner of the room was a door, which led out to a veranda and a garden at the back of the house.

There were no flowers in this tropical garden just a huge expanse of grass that didn't look like English grass and from the veranda were steps leading up to another open space directly above it, where my parents would sit in the evening drinking sweet tea made with evaporated milk. It was easy to climb on the roof from here and run along to the end and frighten the servants.

In Oxford Road there had been only one bedroom, with my parents sleeping in the living room, but in this new house there were two. Each one was very large with unusually high ceilings and electric fans: the walls were painted white and there were no curtains at the windows: instead there were glass shutters. I think that white is an odd colour in the tropics. And my parents slept in one room, and my sisters and I slept in the other. The afternoon and the night were for sleeping.

The furniture was standard issue supplied by the government and brought from England. The beds were called Vono; they were black and made of some kind of metal and there was no vestige of comfort there apart from a thin mattress. My parent's bedroom had shutter doors, which opened onto the back veranda and the garden. Father had a desk in the corner where he worked and wrote. Through the windows where I slept I could see the toilet on one side and the road on the other, and on the road is the KTI or Khartoum Technical Institute.

My mother said I was going to school. She said: "You are going to the Anglican school in Khartoum and it is attached to the Cathedral." She'd been to the market and bought me a little brown case to keep my sandwiches and books in. When it was time to go to the new school she groomed and plaited my hair for a long while, and put olive oil on it, and she said that she'd come with my sisters and me to the school to see that we are all right. She said: "I've arranged it all with the Bishop and he said it was fine and I'll come with you this morning."

So my father drove us our new school, and my mother knocked on the classroom door: she saw, and I saw that it was a white teacher and all the children were white and the walls were white, and when the door opened I saw four or five little white children sat at desks in a small white room. The white teacher looked in horror at my mother and then she looked in horror at the row of beautifully groomed brown children in their new uniforms and their new cases stuffed full with banana sandwiches and said coldly: "We don't have those kind of children here."

This was the kind of thing that my mother couldn't handle: she was fierce and angry and she said she was going to see the Bishop of Khartoum, who was Welsh, and the young teacher was English. She said: "I'm not having anyone talk to me like that and I'm going to see the Bishop." And the very next day the young white teacher was on her way home to England, and my mother was as fierce as that. Then I was sent to another school called Francis Xavier, which was a Catholic School, and I had to start each day in a blue uniform, with PT, which meant physical training, and line up with all the other children in long rows outside the classroom, like we were soldiers. It would be a lesson in Arabic next and I never understood more than a few words, and some I still remember and some I do not.

And in Francis Xavier School we learnt Arabic and I had to trace and copy Arabic letters and learn the numbers on squared paper and some lessons were in English and a little Italian, and lessons began early in the day around seven thirty or eight o'clock; then afterwards the girls waiting for parents would sit and do embroidery. And there were Italian nuns and some of them were cruel and some were not. This was where I learnt to be like my mother. I learnt to sew. I was six.

They were not together; even while my mother and my father lived together, they were not together; even while my father would write love letters to her, it was in a language of a house he didn't enter. And I call this magic. I know this much; that love for many takes a long time, and is not the love that is commonly expressed. It is easier I suppose to say what love was not, than to say what love is. They did not see that the other was themselves, and that everything they saw was just a mirror of themselves. And this is difficult for anyone and requires so much attention. My mother was overwhelmed by him and overwhelmed by her feelings, the ones she could not express and the stories she did not tell. And the stories she does not tell are who she is. And my father, he doesn't do this either, though in Other Leopards he does begin. And he begins because of her; he begins because she is nearer to the reality of her being than he is, because she has to care for the others and she is nearer to herself and her feelings than he is and she is wiser, as a woman is about her emotions, than he is.

But each one overwhelmed the other, and my mother looked after her daughters and in the Mogram house she was the only one: she sewed, she was always sewing and she organised the shopping and she organised the kitchen and she organised the ironing and she was always in the kitchen: and she organised a school and we went to school on Saturday mornings, she organised a Sunday school because she wanted us to have religion which was important to her, but at the same time not at all. She organised for Mr Bob, a white American man to come and collect us on a Sunday morning with his big car and she said:

"On Sunday Mr Bob will come and collect you all and take you to Sunday school and then he will bring you back." And Mr. Bob came and took us to his Sunday school and his car had a great piece of wood down the side and windows to look out and Mr. Bob seemed pleased to see us, but I felt ashamed of being in his world of religion and Sunday schools and whiteness. He had a big house and I didn't go there.

Whiteness is very strange in the tropics, and it looks strange in the sun next to blackness, and it was then I began to notice such things. I noticed the world was divided and there was black and there was white and there were Arabs and Greeks and Coptics and Egyptians and Dinkas and men that came from the desert on camels and the world was all different people. And all kinds of women in long and colourful clothes and shining hair and African children with ripped clothes and no shoes.

Mr Bob came to collect us for his Sunday school and he would drive us into the town; Khartoum it was called and the buildings looked as though the British had been there and his Sunday school was a white timber hut at the front of his house: and his house was huge and his car was huge and it had timber sides. And Mr. Bob taught about God and we sang his songs and one of his songs was:

> *Jesus loves the little children,*
> *All the children of the world.*
> *Red and yellow, black and white*
> *They are equal in his sight.*

I was six, and I was ashamed and I wanted to be a white child and not a brown girl and not have frizzy hair. My mother hated my frizzy hair and she hated my nose, which was like father's and she hated my mouth, which was like father's. And she said I was special and she loved me more than any of the girls. I didn't believe her, like I didn't believe the song or Mr Bob's religion.

And in her daughter she didn't see herself, but she saw him, and in me she saw him and she called me Isabel and that was my father's mother's name, and she called the others Janice and Evelyn and Charlotte and she called me the name of a black woman and she called them the names of white women and there is much power in some names, and in some there is not any.

And my mother didn't sing songs like Jesus Loves the Little Children, she sang Welsh songs, and some of them were called 'Mae gen i dipyn o d bach twt,' which in English was, 'I've got a little house' or something like that, and she sang 'Suo g n' which in English is 'lullaby' . And she was not English and she was Welsh. My father had his own songs and one was called 'Hillang golly rido' or something like that and one was:

> *Dis long time gal me neva see you*
> *Come leh me hol' you han'*
> *(Repeat)*
>
> *Peel neck John Crow sit up a tree top*
> *Eat up de blossom*
> *Come leh me hol' you han'*

And my mother was a transformer, though what might transform herself was more difficult, and she was overwhelming, and home was her life and it was all of her life and her life was religion, and she didn't have a mother and she was going to make a home and she was going to have a mother. And she wanted to be a writer and a poet but more than that she wanted to be mother because she didn't have a mother and she was everywhere being a mother. And everything else she wanted, she put onto my father. Even on the ship or the aeroplane or wherever we were she was being a mother and mothering people and looking after them with great force and richness, and with a heightened morality and as if every mother invaded her spirit. If we were on the plane she was turning over the food and calling the stewardess and if we were on the boat she was in the kitchen and cooking the food, and if it was the stateroom or the shops or the market she was always being and doing what a mother would do and more. She was always fighting for a little quality in life and for things to be done properly.

Once, we were on board an aeroplane and a man was having a fit and he was shaking and no one knew what to do, not even the air hostess, and somehow in an emergency she would wake up and act and she knew just what to do. And my mother came forward and helped the man and she had been a nurse once so she knew what to do. She would wake up and act, but somehow, she was asleep to herself and she could not act, as though her action itself would be against father who was in the driver's seat. And her actions were all about doing for the other and not herself, and this is what she understood by serving the lord. And I have never seen anyone like my mother, because she had true character and soul which is very rare, though I have seen some that come close and some who would be in the running but I have never seen anyone like her.

Chapter Twelve

In which my mother made my father a writer and she made him what he was.

My father was from Georgetown, British Guiana and he was born in 1923. He was brought up as an Englishman, and he was an Englishman. He was a descendant of a slave and his family came from Africa, and though he was African he was not, for he spoke English like an Englishman. He won a British Council scholarship to London where he met my mother: he was doing really well with his art but he was not satisfied. In 1957 he came to Khartoum, which is in the Sudan, and he worked at the KTI, which was the Khartoum Technical Institute.

Every day he rose from bed, he had his breakfast and he took me to the Francis Xavier School and then he went back to his work, which was teaching art history or something like that. I used to watch him when I was not in school: I would stand by the gates of the Mogram house in the shade of the neem tree, and I could just see his head in the classroom in the floors above. And I knew I was like him and I wanted to be near him, but he did not even see me, and when he came home he did not see me either.

In his room I would sit under his table waiting for him to see me, but he did not. His table was covered with papers and he was writing furiously, and he was writing a book called Other Leopards though I didn't know the name of the book he was writing. He didn't see me and I listened to the fan whirring, and watched the green of the hedges muted with the heat, and the grass was parched, and above me I could hear my father and smell him, and I could see his feet. He doesn't talk to me: He is writing the book and he is writing the book through her, for she is the writer. She always said to me: "When I met him he could not write," and she said: "When I met him, he could not write and I taught him to write." And it was my mother who made my father be a writer and it was my mother who taught my father to write.

I remember him walking through the gate and across the sand and through the front door with his journal under his arm: he was walking leaning forward and he was walking quickly as if there were no time or no place for his body. And I remember the sound of it and the regularity of it, and how these things made a frame for a life, like ritual, and that sound was one of them.

He would walk in at the front door and through the darkness of the room, and his feet would make dusty footmarks on the dark tiled polished floor. Then he would enter his room, which was my parent's bedroom, and he would begin to write, as if his life depended on it. And so it did. In his bedroom were two iron beds pushed together and there were double sheets over them and not single sheets. There was no wrinkle in these sheets and no crease.

And I was watching him and waiting but there was nothing, and it took me until now to work out that in that house when my parents were together there was only one. Only one person could be there. If my mother was there, then my father wasn't. He was there, but he wasn't there. And if my mother went into his world there was only one. There was only him in his world. Each of them was the one and not the other, and each of them was overwhelmed by the other. That explains why the accounts of him are so very different to what I remember: I remember a man who was empty and terrifying in his refusal to speak, and respond and take part. Those people who knew him away from home remember enthusiasm, and they remember his passion for learning and Mr Ian Macdonald of the Guyana Sugar Corporation would say at his funeral: "He was overwhelming," and I thought: "How can that be, that he is overwhelming, how can that be?"

My mother was overwhelming because she was not just one mother: she was two in one and I saw the whole pattern of it and the history of it. And I said to myself: "There was only one person in our house, there was only one person: only one person could do this and not the other, and only one person could be a representative and not the other, and only one person could do this and only one person could do that." And if that was the case, which I believe it was, there could only be one winner because the life was a competition to be one. And then I saw my mother and my father was each struggling to be the one and make a place, and which part would I play, and there was only to be one winner and it was to be my father. The winner was only going to be my father or somebody like father. All of this is conformity and competition, and not love, because love is greater and it is not economics, which is important to men and important to women, for when there is plenty of love, there is no competition and there is no conformity and there is no equality. All of these are to do with economics and sex and survival. And competition is struggling to be like someone or somebody who is not you and I think it was a struggle to be like the image of the white man.

There was only one and in the home it was mother, and outside the home it was father, and there was a shortage of love because they couldn't enter each other's worlds and share each other's triumphs and losses which were their own. It was as if black and white could come together and not mix and they lived in separate worlds and each one overwhelmed the other. My father went to work at the college and then he came home and hid in the bedroom, because he had a wife and four daughters and he was overwhelmed by the female.

I never saw my father reading a book, but he had many books and some of them were called Augie March, The Heart is a Lonely Hunter, The Catcher in the Rye, The Leopard, The Group, Light in August, Voss, The Sound and the Fury, Under Milk Wood, Too Late the Phalarope, Last Exit to Brooklyn, Lady Chatterley's Lover, Cry the Beloved Country, Crime and Punishment, The Magic Mountain, The Mandarins, Man's Estate, The Great Gatsby, Miss Lonely Hearts, Day of the Locusts, The Scarlet Letter, Dr. Zhivago, Henderson, The Rain King, The Red and the Black, Short stories by Guy de Maupassant, Amongst the Indians of Guiana, Ulysses, The Ballad of the Sad Café, Invitation to a Beheading, Lolita, The Tropic of Capricorn, The Tropic of Cancer, Giovanni's Room, Another Country, Black Boy, Brother Man, Turgenev's Country Sketches, Life in the Woods, In the Castle of my Skin, The Waste land, Brighton Rock, Pincher Martin, The Naked Lunch, The Naked and the Dead, The Glass Harp, Breakfast at Tiffany's. There were many books and I remember the names of them: they were his books and they were his culture and these were the things that were close to him. I went on the veranda and I taught myself to read and I was six years old and I sat in the hot sun and I amused myself with one book after another and these books were my friends. And when I could read a little, I began to read those books, which were his books, for a child will do anything to be close to father or mother. I read the books, which were his books, and I wanted to be like him and know him because I was him.

He had a Land Rover, not the Rover that he left in London, it was a new Land Rover and it came all the way from London or North Wales or somewhere and it seemed so big and it was grey (like a slate mountain). It had jerry cans on the front and a huge wheel on the bonnet and a canvas roof. The jerry cans held water and spare petrol for when he went in the desert and there were spare tracks on the side for when the Land Rover was stuck in the sand. And it was as a giant plaything and it had doors that came off, and a windscreen that came off and a bonnet that could come off, and a place to sleep in the back under a canvas, which was like a tent.

My mother didn't drive though she did try to learn but father had no patience and he couldn't have her in his world. He would drive us to school and he would drive us back and sometimes he would drive us to the desert to his friends. And he was the driver and he was the person in the driving seat of life and it was symbolic and it was real. Once, many years later someone said of me: "She wants to be in the driver's seat," and I thought what a very odd thing to say about someone, as if most people are happy to be passengers in their own lives.

An Egyptian man, I don't recall his name, though perhaps it was Nassif, and my father would go in the desert, and they would shoot with guns and bring dead animals home. I didn't like it and I didn't want to sit with dead animals in the back of the Land Rover and smell the warm blood or eat them. He called them 'Gazelles', and they were young gazelles and he was excited. I saw them running free and I saw Nassif – he was a big man and they were in his Land Rover with the back removed and they were standing there, all men with their guns. The sun was hot in its usual way and the sand its usual colour, but the sand was made into a storm as they chased after a small herd of gazelles. I was about six then and quite a thin girl with short boyish hair, because my mother wanted me to be a boy. I had a wooden ring back then, a hula-hoop it was called, to play with.

One time my father lost his journal, the one he carried under his arm. It was full of drawings and full of information: I had peeped into it as if it were another world, a secret world: a secret world I wanted and longed to be in and it was full of notes and drawings and it was, as Mr Ian Macdonald of the Guyana Sugar Corporation would one day speak of, the "archive of his mind". And he lost the "archive of his mind" and he drove all through the desert looking for it and never finding it. The black book was gone. The black book was gone but the desert is a very interesting place to be at night: the stars are a great painting in the sky and the sounds of the desert are strange and unworldly and all of that darkness is part of the little girl that I was, and part of my father and mother and my sisters, who were called Janice, Evelyn and Charlotte. And there was no Beatrice back then, and she was still in my mother's belly.

Chapter Thirteen
In which there are separate worlds of brown and white and black.

My father lived in a separate world and my mother lived in a separate world, and we children lived in a separate world, and in our separate world we had to make parents of our own. My father's world was over the road or it was out there, and it was outside and today people talk about 'the real world' and this always makes me want to laugh or at least smile: as if there were separate worlds where there was reality which was owned by them, and some other places which were not real.

And I lived in a separate world because my mother and my father made me separate, and I guess this could be called fragmentation, which means incompleteness and only part of a story and not a whole one. And this fragmentation comes about through power and through fear, and from there not being enough time or enough listening and caring. I am not altogether sure how or why this happens but it happens all the while. I was an outsider in my own family and I wanted to be in but my role in it was not up to me. I was an outsider and my mother was an outsider and I guess my father was an outsider.

I thought my sister Janice was a mother, though she was not a white mother and sometimes I thought my sister Evelyn was a father though she was not a black father, and I'm not sure what I was, since I wasn't a father or a mother and I wasn't black and I wasn't at all white. And we lived in a separate world as if nothing was expected of us, only to be good in the eyes of father, and he didn't expect it of us in any real way for he never entered our separate world of children. In London my mother had bought us books with green covers called The World of the Children and in the Mogram house those same books were there and we were the world of the children. I liked the drawings of the little girl and the little boy who found things out: I didn't like the picture of the boy with scissor hands. And soon I became the

80

boy with scissor hands, the one I was afraid of, I was a mummy's boy and I had done something wrong with scissors in my hands. And I was eternally dammed because I had a rash on my skin and my hair was hard and frizzy and my nose was big like father's and my mouth should stay closed and not speak to father, and I had survived my own death.

In the World of the Children, which was our world, there was play and it was a home made and homespun play and it was a spiritual play and a working out play. We played in the garden and threw rocks at the black birds which sat in the trees, and we played in the water, when the garden was flooded and we played at school, and church with paper dolls: we had services and hymns, and we played at dressing up, and all of our life was play, and we ran along the roof and frightened the servants and that was great fun.

And the white world and the black world and the brown world were all separate from each other, even while there was only one and in the house it was my mother and outside the house it was my father, and nobody met or could meet. And nobody could meet and there was little communication because all the worlds were different colours, and they didn't meet. My mother was literate and she could talk about books and she read Leaves of Grass and it was sitting on her lap, and she read Y Beibl, which was the bible in Welsh and her friend, Lynette had given her that soft backed bible when we went to a Jehovah's Witness meeting in Kent. But my mother couldn't write because there was only one, and only one could be writer, and my father couldn't prepare food because there was only one and my mother couldn't play and my father couldn't play and each world was separate.

And when I returned from Sunday school I would have dinner and then go to sleep for the afternoon because that African sun was too hot, and then go walking near the Nile, along the way of the neem trees, and watch the whole huge sun sinking and the huge moon rising above the water and over the river, watch the darkness descending and smell the fires of the night and listen to the music and drumming. The sound which came out of the darkness was the sound of God and not of man, who can't make anything: and the donkeys would bray and the fires smelt and the night was cool after the hot sun. And once my father took some puppies or some kittens and perhaps it was both and put them in a brown paper bag and he went down the steps by the great river and he threw them into the Nile, and I was there behind him and I saw him, and I said nothing, because I wasn't in his world.

My mother had two servants in the kitchen and one was senior and one was a junior. And Joseph or Adam, I can't quite remember the name, would do shopping and cooking and preparing food, and the boy would do ironing and sweeping and making beds, and we didn't have to make beds or do anything at all. She was in charge of the servants and they also lived in a separate world and they were black and poor. They could buy chickens from the market and they would buy two or three and keep them for a few days and then slit their throats and kill them, and I looked at this and said nothing because I lived in a different world. I would watch them and smell their sweat and I could see the sand on their feet and the dark scars on their flesh, and their washed out limp and faded clothes. They would run after them and kill them and strip them of feathers and pull out their middles and cook them and we would eat them and I would choke on them, and each of us lived in separate worlds.

They kept the innards for themselves after my mother had told them to keep the livers for her. For her they were a delicacy, and kidneys, and she loved frying them in flour and hot butter. And the servants brushed the hot sand with short brushes, and they brushed the sand the next day with short brushes, and the next day they brushed the sand with short brushes, and they killed the chickens and they brushed the yellow sand with short brushes and they lived in a separate and different world.

And play is subversive and it was conforming, and we played at religion and we had little green prayer books, and we played school, and doctors and nurses, and we went to the edge of our world, which was a separate world. And my sister Evelyn who was my mother or my father in our separate world, she had a monkey and it was hers and she was eight years old and I was six years old, and I would soon be seven years old and when I came back to Wales to live I was almost nine years old. My sister Evelyn was exactly two years older and she was born on the self same day of February 21st, the same day as I was and she had a monkey. We were Pisces and my mother said that we were as fish swimming in opposite directions. And she said: "You are each a fish and you do not understand each other because you are swimming in opposite directions," and she, my mother, would talk like that in a strange and symbolic way.

We had a dog – called Boabie – too and we would dress him in little girl's clothes because we were little girls. And he was a scruffy mongrel and he was friendly and he was part of our world. She had a monkey: it was only a small monkey and it was tied to a tree behind the servants' quarters. And she played with it and she wasn't afraid of it as I was, and I was afraid of everything. I was timid and thin and I was always ill with mysterious ailments so that my mother might look after me and love me. And play was subversive because it was having fun, and not work, and it was work that dominated our house: economics and sex and competition and conformity and working. Father is working.

Chapter Fourteen
In which I am frightened of my father and I read his book.

I was in my mother's world but I was not in my father's world
and I was a father in my mother's world. My father did not cook
and he did not shop and he did not do dishes or do ironing or
talk to the servants about rice nor did he do sewing. Yet it was
his work that was important and his life was important and his
pleasure. He was not tall but my mother made him very tall.
And I did not know him though I knew I was him.

I was frightened of him and not just in the usual way; he
instilled a quality of terror into my heart. I could not talk to him
and he could not talk to me. His nose was like mine and his
mouth was like mine. His top lip hung over his bottom lip like
mine, and his hair was hard and frizzy like mine. His skin was
darker and browner than mine, and he was as handsome as I was
beautiful. And he was thin like me. His eyes terrified me and I
would have nightmares about them dripping with blood, because I thought that he would kill me if he ever touched me.

And the boundary of his world was defined by punishment,
a kind of line which said: 'Do not under any circumstances enter
my world, or you will be punished.' And he did punish. And he
didn't want me in his world. His world was for him and it wasn't
for his wife and it wasn't for his daughter. And most of all it was
his voice that petrified me, it turned me to stone and all the time
when I was small I was terrified by people who wore masks
which at small times in Africa made life traumatic for me. I was
frightened of masks and I was frightened of dolls though later in
my life I became interested in dolls. There was a connection;
because my father was to me like someone not alive speaking.

He was writing a book called Other Leopards, which he
dedicated to Katie Alice, which is my mother's name. And it was
published by New Authors Limited and by Hutchinson of
London in 1963. In the note at the beginning of the book it

mentions other writers and some of then are called Stanley Middleton, Julian Mitchell and Elizabeth Mavor. I have heard of Stanley Middleton and I think I met him once in London, though I am not sure. And it also says 'The Company is run on a basis of profit sharing by its authors only', but I do not think my father made any money from this book.

I don't rightly know what my father meant by that Other Leopards; I didn't know if it was a reference to people in his head or some other real people. He talked to my mother then about a book he liked called The Leopard, which was a red book. This Other Leopards book is about a man who is divided and the whole book is about the same thing, about the man who is divided. And the man is called Froad, which is a bit like the psychiatrist and writer, Freud. I didn't read this book until my son, Sam, was at Warwick University many years later, when one day he said to me: "There is a copy of your dad's book here," and I asked him to bring it for me to read because this was a book I did not have. My mother had a copy in our house in Wales but I had not read it. So that was when I read it for the first time, though I was right there when he was writing it.

Anne Walmsley, who is a scholar of Caribbean artists and writers, said in her obituary of my father, she said his book was 'largely autobiographical' and I am sure she is right because she knew my father probably more than I knew him and she knew him in his world and not mine. I heard once that he came to England fourteen times after he left my mother but he never once came up to Wales and I can only suppose that she met up with him then. I have been told though that I am wasting my time thinking it is autobiographical and that I should stick to the facts as if these are the most important.

In his book there is a woman he calls Catherine, which is my mother's name and this woman is his or his boss's secretary, I don't know which; and she comes from a little town in North Wales. She only has a small part in the book and she is the white woman in Froad's life – he also has a black girlfriend called Eve. My father did have a friend called Eve Salahi who was the wife of Ibrahim El-Salahi and they lived as far as I can remember in a traditional African mud house in Omdurman. And the place they lived was very much like the one described in the book. Ibrahim was a student of my father's at the Khartoum Technical Institute and I think he was a calligrapher. There is also a black man called 'the chief' in the book and my father has a friend in Khartoum whom he called the chief.

I am not in the book and my sisters are not in the book and I guess they were otherwise engaged like my Auntie Ethel was at her father's funeral, though he doesn't say so. I would say that most of the book I recognise and some I do not. Some I think has been disguised and in some places the names have been altered. For instance, when he talks about Khutum, that is clearly Khartoum and all the environment he writes about is the same as I remember. I remember his obsession with his writing and I remember his ignoring me and I remember living in Khartoum. I remember his walking in and I remember his walking out and I remember his back more than I remember his front. And he was always writing then, but in London he was always painting. I didn't see him paint anymore like I did in Oxford Road.

And in the beginning of the book it says:

"Denis Williams was born in Georgetown, British Guiana, in 1923. He studied painting at the Camberwell school of Art and from 1950 to 1957 was a lecturer at the Central School of Art, Holborn, and visiting Tutor, Slade School of Fine Art, University College, London and won second prize in the 'Artists under Thirty-five' competition organised by the Daily Express in 1955. From 1957 to 1962 he was Lecturer in Fine Art at Khartoum Technical Institute."

It also said: "At present he is with the Institute of African Studies, University of Ife, Nigeria where he hopes to further his researches in African Antiquity, write and paint," though this whole piece of his life came later.

This was the world he was interested in and this was the world he was successful in and I cannot say he was successful in the other world of my mother or the other world of his daughter or his daughters, though I am sure they do not want me to speak for them, though this is not entirely possible without living in a separate world where I no longer live. And he was successful in his public life and I have never been successful in my public life and I think I have been successful in my private life.

Catherine in the book is learning to drive and he describes her as "...chapel goodness; just right for absorbing my humours. Chapel in the Ogwen Valley, deserted purple quarries... chapel three times Sunday." And she says to him: "Ever wish you were white..."

And he did try and teach her to drive and she was from the Ogwen Valley and the quarries of slate at Bethesda and he did want to be white even while he said he wanted to be black and this was his commitment. And he calls her chicken and he calls her this throughout the book and he says: "Lipstick's not sinful any more these days." He says her eyes were grey, and my mother's eyes are grey and he calls her womb woman and worry woman and he is simultaneously mocking her Puritanism while expressing her as his white meat and good enough to eat.

And my mother did have a thing about lipstick: she had a dressing table drawer full of lipsticks and they were all in different stages of use. They were all either red or pink. She would stand before a mirror and press the pink stuff around her lips and over time it created a strange shape on one side of the lipstick and not the other. Then she would press her lips quite firmly together and rub them about. When the lipstick went down to the base she refused to throw it or waste it and she would pick it out with a matchstick. And I would watch her and resent her keeping all of those lipsticks. And her mouth wasn't big and she always instructed me on how to make my lips small.

I do not like the way my father speaks about Catherine in the book and I do not like the way he speaks of Eve in the book and I do not like the way he speaks of women in the book; I don't care if it's a story or not. I am ashamed of the way he clearly hates women and has no real connection with them, which is much like the way my father was at home. This makes me feel ashamed of him, though it is a feeling I would rather not have. And he speaks of them like a schoolboy, and as if it is a terribly good and important way to speak.

My father also knows a man called the Chief and sometimes in the late afternoon we go to his house and he lives in the town. He is not really called the Chief, he is called Reverend Hamilton and he comes from Georgetown, Guyana, which is the same place as my father. He is bigger than my father, though his skin is the same colour and he is not as handsome and he is religious in a way my father is not. Sometimes we go to see the chief in our Land Rover.

From our home in the Mogram you took the road into town past the prison, which was made of red earth or mud and where the prisoners cried in the night; passed the small shops – which weren't at all like shops in London – where they sold tins of kerosene, and then into town proper. I think there was a Christian bookshop and then the chief lived up some steep steps. There was a roof top veranda to sit and be served coffee in a small tin jug with a long handle and small cups. The night would come quickly and the smells of the fires would rise to this place. And I would sit in this place and wait. Sometimes it was not coffee, sometimes it was very thick dark cocoa, sometimes it was: "Say hello to Hector," which was the chief's son. And once my mother told me that this book was banned in the Sudan. She said: "Denis's book was banned in the Sudan and it was the chief that got it banned because it too much resembled his life and the life of his children."

A man must have a secret life, a kind of invisible life and it must not be known and what must be known are facts and these facts must be indisputable and kind of fixed as matter is fixed. My father wrote that book from his life and then the life is fixed and this is very odd. And what is fixed is true. And all the time he was writing this book I was there. I saw him write with his red Parker pen. He gave me that pen when I was ten and going to the big school, but I lost it that same day and I would never have told him. He finished the book and there were so many manuscripts and some were handwritten and some were not. They were piled up high on his desk. And there was much talk of publishers and rejections and then this book was published, but it was not published when I was in the Sudan.

Chapter Fifteen

In which I find a copy of Other Leopards *in a bookshop in Colwyn Bay.*

My father was always successful in his public life and I can't say that he was successful in his private life. I have said this many times in many ways, for it is very important because it is this division which tormented his life; this division of what is public and what is private, and this division as to what is black and white and this division as to what is female and male. But what he wrote about in his public life was what was private though I'm not sure he saw the contradiction.

And one day around 2003 or 2004 I rode to Colwyn Bay on my bike, which is where his character Catherine comes from and where the Congo boys come from. The story of the Congo boys does come from there, but my mother came from Bethesda. I was coming out of a shopping precinct when I looked over towards the little bookshop. And as I walked towards the bookshop I noticed a small shelf, and books that were only 50p each and then I saw a book by its spine only and I recognised it as my father's book. It was Other Leopards.

And I picked it up and I thought I noticed the smell of the pages and the print, though it was just the dried up paper, and I recalled my old fears for him and that old life and I felt my fear and my childish excitement as though I were still a child. I reached inside my purse for the right money and I went inside the bookshop, which was quite dark.

I said to the bookseller, I said: "This is my father's book!" I said with this childish excitement and I said: "I didn't have a copy and now I have!"

Then I gave him the book, which was called Other Leopards, and he looked at the front and in the front cover – it was a first edition and then he looked at the back where there was a small photo of my father with a beard. And I said: "Look that is him in the photo!" But he continued to inspect the book as if he was searching for some evidence of value, which he might have overlooked, but it didn't mean anything to him and then I said: "He used to live here in Wales!"

But what I said was no use for he hadn't heard of him and he hadn't heard of that book and it wasn't much use getting all enthusiastic with no-one at all to share it with. Then I rode back to Llandudno, where I live now and I was thinking how strange it was to come across that book like that and how life was such a strange thing as if it were an adventure leaving clues and things all over the place. I rode past some of the places we had stayed as children and they were the tall red-bricked buildings near where there was a small church on the beach. And I rode past the old toll bar and passed Batty's and all the time I was thinking about him and the book in my bike basket.

And all that memory came flooding back like water, without resistance and memories and images and words. I remembered that terrible fear and all the great insignificance of memory and even words themselves: then I wanted to write something and I wrote an essay called His Master's Voice. It was his voice I could not integrate and it stuck out there as though on a stick; ah a voice and what might I do with a voice!

I thought about his journal and the way it made him walk in a certain way, like the journal itself gave importance, a book full of words and scribbles and drawings. And some of the words were in English and some of the words were in French. I thought of the old Mark's carrier bag of my mother's writing which had her scribbles and her poems and things that weren't at all fancy. I thought of the night when we were returning from El Obeid or Shendi or some such name and when he realised he had lost his journal, how he rode through the night, and that very blackness, but he never found it.

I thought about how I was a little girl looking like a boy and how I would go and sit under his desk so as to be like him with the vain hope that he would speak to me and how I would cuckoo down in the noisy silence and listen to the thunder of the typewriter above me and the constant whirr of the ceiling fan above me and the warm air being reluctantly pushed about. I would stare beyond the veranda doors out to the garden which was called a compound and where my sister would ride on our servant's bike. He had bought that Smith Corona typewriter, second hand, from a friend. He was terribly excited about this machine and it signalled a new development in his career and the beginning of a literary journey. And before this time he had completed one manuscript by hand, and then another. His papers were always piled up on his desk, which as a child seemed so out of reach.

And this book is full of his uncertainty about who he is, and he is preoccupied with who he is and he is questioning all that he knows and so many questions are his concern. I remembered my mother saying that his own mother had made him trousers made of sugar sacks and how that had affected him and marked him as these things do; as the black and white clothes my mother finds in the attic at Cefnfaes Street affected her. And this is the image he carries and cannot escape from.

Then I went home and I began to write and then I wrote an essay about the book and I sent it to Mr Ian Macdonald in Guyana and he said he might publish it in a magazine called Kyk over al, but later that wasn't possible. He introduced me to an editor of another journal who said she would publish it, but in the end I withdrew it. And at that time, which was quite some years after my father's death in Georgetown, he was being made into a kind of cultural hero of the Guyanese people.

At the same time another book came into my life and that was called In Sir Vidia's Shadow and I happened upon that in my own library and in that book was a story about a man like my father and the name of that man was V. S. Naipaul. I had many times heard my father speak about Naipaul with my mother though I did not know what he was saying at all. For as he spoke he mentioned many famous people and some of them he mentioned as if they were his friends.

My father spoke of 'Baldwin', who is James Baldwin and Carew, who was Jan Carew and Dathorne, who was Ronald Dathorne and he was always speaking about artists and writers like they were all mates together. I guess this was where I got the idea that you could write to writers as mates and I had already begun to do that. And sometimes they would respond and sometimes they would not.

And the person who had written the book I found was called Paul Theroux and I had never heard my father mention him. I could not help noticing the similarities between Naipaul and my father, so I was beginning to think of something like a Caribbean character or something like that. I had my essay and my usual way of writing to authors, so I sent my essay to him and then with all of these things I quite forgot about it.

As I had forgotten about my letter to Paul Theroux, it came as a pleasant surprise to see that he had written to me. To my surprise he said that he had known my father in Uganda in 1966 and that he had given him and my mother a lift from a party. This is something of what Paul T. said. He said:

"You are right to compare him to Naipaul – though Naipaul never met him in Uganda. These two men were competitive (both in their mid thirties but speaking across a racial divide)." And then he told me a story about my father.

"Once I gave him a lift from a party (at Rajat Neogy's – editor of Transition Magazine). I asked him what he was planning to write about. He said, "Wheels." This seemed far-out to me. I thought: Wheels of fortune? He had to repeat this four times before I (with my American tin ear) realised he was saying "Wales" in his West Indian accent. He got very irritated having to repeat it."

Chapter Sixteen

*My father has soft hands and not hard hands and his hands are
brown and a darker shade of brown to mine and my father is a
Victorian.*

My hands are scarcely brown at all. The way he behaves is like a
Victorian and Victorians believed that children were to be seen
and not heard and many other quite contradictory things. I have
heard that his father was like this. He went to London and then
he went to Africa and then he went back to Guyana.

And in slavery his name was Williams and the Williams's had
been slaves and they were owned by white people and they
forgot their land and they forgot their name and they forgot
their religion and they forgot their culture and all the things that
made their home. In slavery the Williams's were owned by the
white woman and the white man who gave them that name, and
they belonged to the slave owner, and the slave owner owned
them. The 'who do you belong to' was broken and fractured, and
a man and a woman who were married did not belong to each
other, a man did not belong to a woman and a woman did not
belong to a man: a child did not belong to a mother and a child
did not belong to a father. In slavery the Williams's belonged to
a slave master and a slave master could sell the Williams's.

And I did not know about his mother, though I was named
after her; I did not know her and I did not know about slaves
from him and I did not know of a black history from him and I
did not know what his home was like from him. I do know that
what a mother does is make a home and I do know, though not
from him, that my grandmother liked to garden and make quilts
as I do.

What I do know is that his mother made a home and directly
or indirectly this home was a home for the image and culture of
the white man and the life as it is to be lived and called real. I
smile: for what is real is competition and what is real is money

and what is real is conformity and what is real is exploitation, and what is good is the image of the white man and the whole life is for the white man. And it is the white man who plays at being god and who plays at being this huge and external authority. And what is homely is simultaneously not real. And the language she teaches her son is for the white man, and for this life that is real. And his rage is against her and his origins and his rage is for the image of the white man who is his mother who made him. And this I know because I knew my father. And this intimacy of language, which she taught him, is both liberation and oppression; this language is a house, which is not a home. My father's house is huge and monumental and solid as a castle.

To make a language into a home is a matter of some difficulty even while it is easy. And to be colonised is to find that everything is for the white man and everything my father did was for the white man and his sense of homelessness comes out of that and his fugitive slave-self came out of that. For language is to express relationship between people and there were many different people and races in Guyana, and as in slavery the relationships were broken and the families were broken and expressions of true feeling were impossible because everything was for the white man, measured by the language of the white man, because of slavery. And words were spoken according to the rules and according to white culture and what was the right thing to say, and father was always looking for the right words and the right intimacy and he didn't find it because it was against the rules.

And the rules were, do not express your feelings, do not complain against injustice and do not complain about oppression and do not complain about slavery and do not complain about history, even while it is alive in your heart. The white man doesn't like complaints: so there was no talking back and there was no resistance: so what does my father mean and what does my mother mean? And a mother meant nothing in slavery and a father meant nothing in slavery and a child meant nothing in slavery, for when value is put on economics and sex, then a mother ceases to have value and she has no meaning, and it doesn't matter what she does, it would have no meaning. And politics is destructive of meaning and pursuing money is destructive of meaning and seeking power is destructive of meaning and competition is destructive of meaning. And exploitation is destructive of meaning. And slavery is destructive of meaning.

So all emotional attachments are for the master and what is important is the master and what he wants, and this is the pressure of life and feeling at home would be feeling attached to something which is a bind and which is slavery. And what is freedom? It is not being ruled by fear and desire, by fear and wanting: my father finds it difficult to be affectionate and his fear of loosing his freedom enslaves him. And my father has no problem with wanting but wanting is his problem and to be ruled by the desire of others was his greatest fear; so he doesn't want what he wants and he wants what the other wants, and he is always looking in the other for what he wants and the other is important, but only as an other. And he cannot enter a relationship with the other because they, which he doesn't want, would rule him.

And my mother is Welsh, and Wales was ruled by the English, and her parents were ruled by the English, and all those Hughes's before them were ruled by the English, and every relationship was bound by the English; and the schools and the hospitals and the laws. And what is good is English and what is good is the image of a white English man and what is considered serious is English. And what is bad is English and what is exploitative is English. And what is scholarly is English. And Welsh was a language that was censored, and my mother's voice was censored. And this history lives on in the heart of a man and in the heart of a woman and in the heart of a child. My mother tried to escape from Wales and being Welsh because she didn't have a mother, and she felt homeless, and she left Wales and she went to Africa, but everywhere she went she was still Welsh, the Welsh she was always running away from. Then she went to Africa to get away from her mother who was Bethesda and Wales but she always took her mother with her. And my mother was always bound by the desire she didn't want and she could not be free because she always wanted what she didn't want.

My mother was Welsh and when she went to school she spoke English and she spoke her Welsh in English and she couldn't speak Welsh to her daughters, who were not Welsh. And power and money is destructive to language and meaning and communication and my mother was not at home speaking Welsh and she wasn't at home speaking English and she didn't speak Welsh to her daughters.

My father was a Victorian, a fact he couldn't get away from and one of the main things about a Victorian is his good name and to keep a good name was, I'm sure, a full time occupation and it is, I know, the subject of Bleak House. How I love that title! A bleak house is where the most important thing of all is to maintain a good name. That is such a hard thing to do and it demands no end of secrecy and no end of not going into secret rooms and not going into secret gardens. It demands what is commonly called loyalty, which of course is not loyalty and it demands honour; an honour which is of course dishonour.

My father is a Victorian and he can do no wrong and he must not be seen to be doing wrong and he must be seen to be rational where his morality is not in question. He must be seen at the head of the table (my mother must not) and driving the car; (my mother must not) and be cultured (my mother must not) and have language (my mother must not): for somehow a man must be more than he is, he must be put upon and he is expected to act like a man.

And my mother was in the kitchen and she was telling the servants how many times to wash rice and how to pick it over and take out all the bad grains and the rotten grains and all the small stones and to put just enough water so that it did not boil dry, how to clean a chicken and how to cut it and how to dip it in flour and fry it in hot fat and that sort of thing. She was there laying out the old blanket for ironing and inspecting how much coal was in the iron and whether it was hot enough and what kind of meat the servants had bought and have they swept the floor and all things like that.

I remember the heat and the sun and the noise and the traffic, the brown skin men in their long gowns and their perfume smells and the social tension and the tension in my father and the silent tension in my mother absorbed into her silent sewing. My mother, she looks like some Hedy Lamarr or better still a Barbara Stanwyck, almost, but not quite a burlesque figure: the way of the walk, the way of the talk, an imitative sexuality with her pale face and red lipstick. My father's mask and my mother's mask – they are not real characters but my mother is closer to the possibility of freedom and she is closer to the heart of pain.

And that was my mother's life in Khartoum, and my father's life was writing his book and that was his life. And my father's life was the car and public life. And a man must bear all of that and yet be silent. He must be silent and hold the line, for this is the nature of a man. And in the rooms that you don't see and in the rooms that my father couldn't see and in the rooms that no one went into or talked about, was a mumbling sadness that had no home and no language to say... and all this made for incompleteness, which is the nature of fragmentation. And the society is fragmented and it is called a real world. And when people talk about the real world as they do, it makes me smile a sad smile that has no words.

But father was raised in the white tradition, and in England, which is full of white people, he is a black man and he is not a white man, and in Africa, which is full of black people, he is not a black man, so my father does not know what he is. He is aware of the contradiction, which is himself; he is aware that he is not the black of Africa and he is not the white of English and this awareness is terrifying as it is lonely and he finds himself alone with his division. And division is torment and conflict because how can you go on a journey when you are pulled in two directions at once, and how can you do anything at all – really do anything – when you do not know whether you are a black man or a white man. It was not Africa that made him like this and it was not London that made him like that, but it is power and colonialism and the empire and the images and the culture of white people.

It is said that if you spend the night on Cader Idris you will see God or you will become mad. And my father was not mad, but he had stared right into some ineffable blackness and it had changed his life. He ran and ran to separate himself from this blackness, and from Lobo and from his dark mother and his dark daughter and his white goddess. He saw reality and it was too big for him, the mysteries in life and in death. He went into the cave and he spent the night there, the cave he began to paint in, and he saw something in that illuminating darkness and his consciousness was fractured, broken like a nut's hard casing. The roof fell in and he and his friend nearly died, and then he saw something; his own mortality perhaps and that is why he went to Africa. Something happened and he went to Africa and Africa was a place of uncertainty and not a place of rest or peace, though it might have been.

In Africa, the image of his self is threatened and every black man threatens his sense of self, and every white person. He has gone to Africa, like some Victorian explorer, like Speke or Burton or Livingstone, like a white man, to find a place by a river, a place where black people live and work and die. And the river is like the quarry, a place of work and a place of beauty and history and a place of witness as nature is a witness.

He went to the Nile to find the source of civilization, and to find himself there, and when he was there, he found that he was a stranger, and that he was not a black African and he was not a Muslim and the people he thought were his brothers were not his brothers and the women he thought were his sisters were not his sisters. He was seeking relationship and authenticity, and he was seeking community and he was writing a book and the book was about him, though it is disguised. I am standing by this, because in some strange way I understand it, I recognise it. I see him and I hear him. I am a little girl at his feet and he is writing furiously and he is writing obsessively and that is how I know. He is in the air and his writing is in the air and I absorb him.

Chapter Seventeen

In which we go to live near the gates of Cwmdonkin Park.

In the spring of 1959 my mother goes back to Wales with the Yules's to have the baby that is in her belly. And the Yules's were a family who lived near us in the Mogram. My mother said she was going back to Wales. She said: "I am going to Swansea to have a baby and I will be going there with the Yules's and you will stay with your father and you will come later." She said: "I will get us a house first and I will have a new baby and then you will come to Swansea." So in 1959 my mother moved to Swansea with the Yules's and then my father moved to Swansea and my mother had her new baby and we stayed in a large house near Cwmdonkin Park. Before we came from Khartoum my mother was involved in a car accident with the Yules's but she was not hurt. One of the Yules's children was called Poppy and she was as white as the sun.

The Reverend Hamilton came to our house in the Mogram and he brought with him a huge tin bowl of buckwheat porridge because my mother had left for Wales. He always tried to look after us as a family and he remembered our birthdays, which he had written in a little book. One time he bought me a mother of pearl new testament and I still have this today. My mother wrote a little poem inside it, which said: "Sing a song in this garden of life, if only you gather a thistle, sing a song as you travel along, and if you can't sing, why just whistle."

My mother bought me a red cloak with a big black velvet bow from a charity shop that summer and she sent me to school to Sketty Junior School with my sister Evelyn. And we went back and forwards to the Sketty School on a bus and I with my red cloak on and hating my mother and she bought me johnny shoes though I didn't know what they were.

The house in Cwmdonkin Park was on three levels, I think, and the trees were just coming into green leaf and there were many trees there. And my father came to the school and he came to my class and it was the beginning of the summer and he had on a black Aquascutum suit and he was clasping his hands behind his back like royalty and he came to my class and I had to speak to him. The way he walked into that class was odd as though he were acting a part and I was terrified of him who was part of me. I just froze in my place and I wanted to die, but my teacher said I had to say good morning Mr. Williams or something like that. So I said: "Good morning, Mr. Williams."

My father locked me and my sister in a bedroom to learn the eight times table and I couldn't learn it and I stared out of the window and watched who went through the gate of Cwmdonkin Park and I watched the rain drops running down the telegraph wires. I often did this when I was young because I thought it was fun. When he unlocked the door he said: "Do you know your tables?" And I said no. Then he would go away and then try again; but I never did learn my tables this way.

Then my mother said that Auntie Maggie was coming and she came to that Swansea house. And when she came she said that her husband Matt who was a builder was working for Tyldsleys in Craigydon, and she said: "There are some new houses being built in Maenan Road by Griff Roberts." I'm not at all sure of the surname but it was something like that. She was enthusiastic as she always was and she knew my mother wanted a home more than anything in the world. And it was decided then and there to go to North Wales. And that is how I came to live in North Wales and not South Wales.

So soon after my mother had her baby who was called Beatrice Emma after one of her friend's Lynette's names we came to North Wales. And she was born in June. And when we got there father was still wearing that suit, the one that frightened me in the Sketty School. He was wearing a suit and he was walking through Craigydon Park in the summer of 1959, which was the same summer my youngest sister was born. He was all stiff, like a dead man, with his hands knotted behind his back as if the most important thing in life was to make your body look as though it had no feeling. And he was walking like he was at some kind of funeral, all formal and stiff and terrifying and he was walking with Mr Roberts who was a quite elderly man wearing a sport's jacket and plain trousers and a tie. And this image makes me sad because it is sad and Mr Roberts was an elderly gentleman, with white hair who had a more than passing interest in local history and they were talking together and I was looking at them through the little window of my Auntie Enid's and my Uncle Walter's terraced cottage which was and still is, in Craigydon, near the paddling pool, the beach and the tennis courts.

Father was studying all he could about the Congo boys and he was excited as a young boy, like when he would find African dolls in the market place. He is excited because he thinks that the Congo boys might be him or his ancestors come to Wales and that he now must have a place because they had a place.

But all the time he was keeping his tail cool; he would often say this: "Keep your tail cool," which is just what he said about excitement. He used to say: "Keep your tail cool and be sharp." He was studying the Congo boys with Mr Roberts and they were walking in the park together near the tennis courts and the old pavilion, where later I would go to a ballroom dancing lesson with Glenys Jones, whose father owned the Clark's shoe shop in Craigydon. And they went together to Colwyn Bay where the African men had been buried and they looked at the graves as if they were the custodians of the dead. And at this time my father was still writing Other Leopards and he brought Mr Roberts into the story of Other Leopards and he made him Catherine's father. And my real mother's father was called John William Hughes.

My father never lived in Llandudno, though my mind and my imagination likes to think so, likes to place him there in a story in my mind; a story, like a play with parts where I could be and he could be, and mother could be and I could even play out the role as a character in that play and all of that. How strong are stories and imagination and how strong was the play, and all the parts in it. If I lived in Bethesda I could play at being with mother and if I lived in Llandudno I could play at being with father and I was looking for a home too and not finding one; and it took me a long time to see that looking for a home is futile and its very worth is in its failure and not its success.

He was there in the summer of 1959, and he was there in my mind, and behind him was the granite mountain, a great image of security of nature, a mountain that had always been there and would always be there. And I have heard that he was jealous of my mother's land as he didn't feel he had a land like she did. That summer marked the real end of us as any kind of family and we were never a family again, as a family is that live together and talk together and stayed in the same house together.

He was still working in Khartoum then and that was 1959 and he had been there from 1957, when he came from London and we had all been there with him until then. He went back to Khartoum, which is in the Sudan, and what followed afterwards was ten years of travel between Wales and Africa, travelling to see father and him travelling to see us and, our new home wasn't a home at all. And it was called Beit-eel, which meant house of god.

Chapter Eighteen
In which my mother has her first new house.

The same summer my mother and my father bought a semi detached house at the end of Maenan Road near the farmer's fields and near to Cwm mountain. We did not have any furniture so she a bought a new cooker, a stainless steel kettle and some wool blankets and an iron. My mother bought a grey bed settee from a shop in Craigydon and she bought two double beds and a single bed; she bought woollen blankets and she bought a large electric cooker, which was called a Tricity Bendix or something like that. And she bought six wooden chairs with curved tops and a second hand table and sideboard. We had an old wooden kitchen table in the kitchen which Auntie Enid gave us and Auntie Maggie gave us the corner piece of her kitchen units; the bit that didn't fit in her house and it didn't fit in ours either. It was a useless and ugly piece of kitchen furniture that my mother would not dispose of saying that we had nothing to replace it with.

Our new house, Beiteel, was a modern semi-detached house. It had a glass front door and a small sitting room and a small dining room that was one through room. The kitchen was small and upstairs were three bedrooms and a bathroom and a separate toilet. Above the separate toilet was a trapdoor to the attic. At the front of the house was a garden and at the back of the house was a garden. Behind our house were many other houses with gardens.

Auntie Maggie came there with her bargains but they were gifts of shame and my mother bore the shame and she would always have to pay twice; once for the goods, whatever they were – ancient armchairs which didn't fit the small rooms; in fact nothing she gave us fitted our life and my mother she would pay again by carrying the shame of her poverty and hardship.

My mother bought an Indian carpet and she was cleaning it

all the time and there was a dreadful quality about that; an endless cleaning which didn't clean. And she bought a pale blue Ewbank and she would be cleaning that carpet all the time. She had a dustpan and brush, which were always in her hand, and she was always washing it and making it clean. And this is what she was like; cleaning all the time and washing clothes in the bath and washing sheets in the bath because we didn't have a washing machine and she was cooking and cleaning the yard and she was cleaning the carpet, which was the only one we had then. And this cleaning and cleaning and cleaning made me sad and kind of desolate.

The floors of the house had a mustard coloured lino, which was cold and freezing in winter. At the front of the house was a garden but more it was a patch of green sloping towards a front wall that my father had made into two levels. It should have had flowers growing there and bushes and bulbs for the spring but it didn't. And in the back of the house was an even larger patch of green and it was for my mother a space she could not manage. And it might have been a garden with flowers and vegetables like the man next door. But it was not like this. There were no flowers there and my mother would come out of the kitchen every now and then and cut the grass with her bread knife. I always thought this was a quite normal thing to do: I had seen our servants in Africa do this with a larger knife and it didn't seem at all odd to me. Many years later I would do the same thing myself because I learnt many things from my mother.

And every morning she would get up and she would have a cup of tea, which was 'cwpanaid o de' in Welsh. She liked to put the tea leaves in the bottom of the cup and cover them with boiling water. The tea would be dark and strong and thick and it was PG Tips or Glengettie tea and she would suck on the tea leaves and draw her lips out, so as not to waste the taste. Halfway down the cup she would top up her beverage with hot water and begin again.

And she would separate the cream from the milk and put it in a little pot jug and use this for her tea. Later she bought a stainless steel teapot, second hand and a stainless steel milk jug and a stainless steel sugar bowl and I bought her a red and white Royal Albert china cup because she only liked to drink tea from china and not pot cups. And her teacup had brown stains in it from the tea.

And when she got up in the morning she would take a bath in an inch of water which she made very hot because she wouldn't mix it with cold water and she would always get in the bath quickly so as not to let the water go cold. I would hear her and she would say: "Aaah!" and it was the pain of the hot water on her feet and the sound came through her gritted teeth, like with her tea.

And almost as soon as she went in the bath she was out, and there was no hanging about or enjoying herself or anything like that, and her body was not for enjoyment it was for work. Then she was out and she was rubbing herself hard dry: she didn't like soft towels, and then she would call me and ask if I wanted her water to wash in and I liked to wash in her water because by that time it would be deliciously warm and all soapy with Fairy soap or red soap and occasionally it was Lux soap flakes.

She would dress in the same old woollen dress that she'd bought in Marks, a dress she had routinely darned and then she would go downstairs and begin to clear out the grate. If I was lying in bed I could hear her. She would pull out the front of the fire and it would make a terrible noise and she would clear all the ashes from underneath the fire basket and put them in a sheet of newspaper. We never got newspapers so I don't know where they came from and she would wrap the ashes like her father I suppose had wrapped parcels in his shop.

Then she took her red handled broom which was about twenty four inches long and she would thrust it up the chimney and I could see her white skin and her pink rubber gloves: her marigold hands were urgently seeking the soot and there was a quality strange and urgent about her relation to dirt, like when she cleaned the carpet. And when the cleaning of the chimney was complete she would pull out the grate and all the different and separate items that made up our fireplace. She would sweep and collect the ashes, wrap them up in newspaper and take the neat package she had made to the dustbin.

She never asked for help with the housework and I wanted to Ewbank the carpet or do the shopping and I tried to help her and I did help her but she didn't want help. And sometimes I would sweep the stairs or when she was tired of working for all of us she would complain how we didn't help her. She would say: "You treat me like a dog," and in the end nothing counted and that was the worst; nothing counted, only what she did.

She was always noisy doing that job of the fire as though she were trying to say something else, something she could not say and I hated the noise she made when she banged on the pressure cooker. She was angry but she couldn't say it. Then, she would put the tablecloth on the table, and the tablecloth was kept in the sideboard in the second drawer down. In the first drawer was the bone cutlery, which you weren't allowed to immerse in water. And there was a glass decanter for the wine we didn't have and the green glasses and the green jug, which were for the visitors we did not have.

My mother wouldn't let anyone do the dishes either, and she complained that I didn't do anything. She used to say that washing up was the hardest job in the house and this was her virtue and her smallness and her arrogance; that she was the only one who could do the mundane jobs.

My mother smoked and the cigarettes she smoked were called Embassy. Sometimes if she didn't have much money she smoked Player's No.6 and sometimes she just bought five because you could then. In the Sudan she had smoked Craven A. When my father came home from the Sudan he smoked Player's Plain and sometimes he smoked Player's Navy Cut and sometimes he smoked a pipe. I hated my mother smoking because it made me remember what I really felt inside but she never did stop.

And she was always busy and it was hard and almost impossible to get to know her. I would sit and wait and watch her and I remember her cooking bacon and eggs; it was almost as hard to get to know her as my father. We had a lot of eggs back then and I can remember some of the meals we had with regularity. And some of these meals were: roast lamb on Sunday and left over lamb with beans on Monday, chips and egg on Tuesday, breast of lamb on Wednesday; at the end of the week it was spaghetti Bolognese.

And she really liked bacon. She would send me to the corner shop which was over the field where the houses were not as yet built; there was a rough path back then which cut between the farmer's fields. She would say: "Isabel, go and get two slices of bacon and put it on the book." And I would go over the field and ask Mrs Denis, the lady who owned the shop to cut two pieces of bacon on No.5, which was the right number for the machine to cut the bacon for my mother. She wouldn't have any other cut. And if the bacon weren't right she would make me take it back.

When we had bacon she would grill it slowly so it didn't crisp too much. She would cut up the two pieces with a scissors into six pieces, and she would say: "I've cut it thin so you all got a taste." And an egg of course, from the man at the door, along with lots of white bread toast cut in the Welsh way. She would turn the white tin loaf into an upright position and spread it with melted butter and cut it ever so thinly and finely. She was an expert in this: when she made toast she turned the loaf and cut it thicker.

And it was almost impossible to get to know my mother because she had so many jobs to do. She always said that washing up was the most important job in the house. She said: "Washing up is the most important job in the house." No one else could do washing up like her, or cleaning like her and she did the washing up like she did her sewing, as though she was in fact praying. She stacked up all the dishes neatly and sometimes she rinsed them first and then she would wash each plate and rinse each plate and each piece of cutlery was individually washed and the bone handle not placed in the water. She would place all the cutlery on a dry tea towel to be dried and put away. And she was immersed in this separate world of prayer. And she would send me on shopping errands and I was always pleased to go to get bread or mincemeat. And she would say: "Take 2/6 from my purse and go to Needham's and Dunphy's and these were the names of the bread shops in Craigydon.

There was a hidden tyranny that limited her life and limited it to certain fixed boundaries and this was a tragedy and I am asking myself is this something that men do to women and is it something that my father did to my mother or was it just something they fell into because of the wider culture? And there is no doubt that my mother was oppressed and held within certain boundaries and that she couldn't express her life and my father could not express his life. And she also held herself in tight boundaries, as did my father.

Chapter Nineteen

In which my father meets a man in the Sudan and he is called Ulli Beier who likes him and finds him a new job in Nigeria.

As I said it was a matter of desire and who had what and who could say what and all that kind of thing and all the things were quite split up and categorised; and it all quite depended on who you were in the scheme of things, just like an organisation might be and some rules that were hidden and some rules were not.

Food was for my father and writing was for my father and talking was for my father and the life was for my father and not my mother. Talk was for my father and words were for my father and it was a patriarchal voice that was to be heard. My mother's voice was not to be heard unless it was mediated through my father as there could only be one voice. The authentic voice of my mother was lost and only faintly heard, though truthfully this also happened to my father. His voice was not to be heard.

And voice is as layers and layers, like the very ancientness of slate, and a true voice of joy and pain and rage was never heard. What was individual had to be drummed out in service to the voice of power and the right thing to say. And the right thing to say was often nothing at all and this was the legacy of colonialism and this was their life. Do not have feelings and do not have a body and if you have feelings keep them in private and do not mix the private and the personal.

In Wales I was sent to Craigydon school and then I went to big school and it was called John Bright's. My father sent me a telegram and it said well done for passing your scholarship or something like that; but I hadn't taken a scholarship, because there wasn't one, so I didn't pass it. But I didn't care because he came home and he bought me the best present ever which was a Palm Beach bike from Orme's Cycles in Llandudno. And having a blue bike meant that I could get away from the house, which is what my parents had trained me to do. I rode all over the place and some of the places were Conwy and Penmaenmawr and Colwyn Bay and up to the woods at Gloddaeth Hall, which was a girl's boarding school.

My father's book Other Leopards was published and it, the green book, arrived in the new house in Llandudno, which was called Beiteel, which meant house of god. Until 1962 my father worked in the Sudan and he moved from the Mogram House to a smaller house in the north of Khartoum and it was called Shambat. And we all lived in Wales now and visited my father only and he visited us only and we didn't live like a whole family again. That was all over. And most of this time after this was now spent with my mother's relatives.

I never did like Beiteel as a house and I did not consider it a home and I thought it to be an empty edifice and a symbol not of their relationship but of their lack. And this is the way I thought, though I did not think it then. There was fun there and there was excitement and there was so much sadness that I saw in the life. And for the next ten years or perhaps much less my mother would travel backwards and forwards to Africa and to my father and she would take my two youngest sisters with her. And they were called Beatrice and Charlotte and the three eldest were called Evelyn Janice and Isabel. And it was a lonely and isolating existence whilst having no privacy and the life was continually watched and watched and watched.

And in 1959 I went to school in Craigydon and I was in Mr. Roberts's class and my father had moved to Shambat in the north of Khartoum, and then I was in Mr Thomas's class and then in 1961 I went to John Bright School. And then Other Leopards came out and I was in the second form in 1962 and 1963. And all the way up the school my father wasn't there and most of the time my mother wasn't there. And when my parents were there they were not there. My father was always in the bedroom and he was always typing and what I could hear was the typing. He was cold when he came home, though it was often summer and when he would finish typing then he would watch cricket and he was mad for cricket and West Indians and all of that.

But he wouldn't let us watch telly and Sunset Strip or whatever it was we were watching just then: he would only let us watch circus or something we were not interested in. And I hid behind the sofa, as I would do in Africa sometimes because I wasn't allowed in his world. Race was never mentioned and sex was never mentioned though he once gave us a lecture when he heard us saying queer. But I didn't even know what queer was when he was giving us a lecture.

And because I was like him and reading books all the while, he asked me to go to the library and fetch his usual books. And the writer he was interested in was called Samuel Beckett; then I would go to the library on my bike and get this huge book; the library was quite different in those days and I loved to be there.

In Khartoum in1962 he met a man called Ulli Beier, a German man, who invited him to work in Nigeria. And it was Ulli who found him a job in a new university called the University of Ife. And Ulli and my father are interesting men and they met in Khartoum and my father went to work in Nigeria in the University of Ife. Ulli had begun the Mbari, which was a kind of workshop for artists, and writers and he had started two magazines and one was called Black Orpheus and one was called Odu. And he set up art workshops and drama workshops and my father was part of this in small ways. And these two men are interesting because they were looking at the same situation in Nigeria but from different points of view.

And my father was a black man from Guyana and Ulli was a white man, a German Jew who had to leave Germany and they are both looking for a place to be. They are both interested in the power of Africa and the art of Africa and they are both fascinated by the cultural traditions of Africa and they are both, a white man and a black man, caught up in a tradition of Africa.

113

And both of these men value art and creativity and what they see in Africa are "stereotypes" and African art is important because of the rejection of the individual.

And my father goes into the rules and he goes into the richness and he goes into the traditions and he is fascinated as to where it has come from and where he has come from. And Ulli is doing the same thing and they are both displaced people looking for a place and they both try to preserve Africa and own it and claim it in a very western way.

And in doing so they safeguard authority and western thinking and they encourage African artists and this very encouraging changes the culture they love so much; in the Mbari, Ulli is the authority on what good art is. And this way of looking which is western is contrary to the tradition of Africa, which is or was undivided and not individual creativity.

And Ulli is a connoisseur and an inspirer and he comes from a rich cultural background and my father comes from a "culture-less" background and they are both looking for authenticity – the real thing and in a way they both betray it because of their own fragmentation and their own dividedness.

And my father begins to write another book and to research another book called Icon and Image, which details the sacred art of Africa. He needs a history, because of slavery and he needs a history and he has no route back to Africa and no images. And his concern is for community and for memory and for ancestry; for without community there is no art. And there are no writers.

And Ulli himself has a culture but because of his Jewish-ness he is estranged from his birthplace in Poland and Germany. On the surface they seem to be interested in the same thing and the same wish for culture and Ulli sees creativity in terms of individual expression and he is keen to promote black people and he is keen to promote my father and many years later he is keen to promote me. And my father is looking for a body, a body of knowledge and Ulli already has a body of knowledge and he seeks to liberate the mind, the individual mind of African art through individualism and neither of them looking is complete. Complete is hard and arduous, but necessary because of the burden of memory and facts and all of that.

My father began writing Icon and Image in Africa and my mother was in Wales in her Beiteel, her home which was named by "the chief", Reverend Hamilton. She was at home with her five daughters or she was in Africa with her husband and with two daughters or she was travelling the seas and holding her family together this way. My father wasn't writing Other Leopards anymore and he was writing a book that was later called "magisterial" and monumental and pioneering. This book is difficult and I was not able to read it or maybe only the first page and a few others. There are no Africans in it though it is about Africans. And what it is, is analysis and form and data and stuff like that which is very much a European way of looking at things and at life. It is masculine and it is linear and it is as one-dimensional as writing could possibly be as if there were no space for anything or anybody else and there are no others and no other leopards.

My father desired embodiment and Mr Ulli Beier desired embodiment and they both sought it in the African and it was this desire that made for my father's dynamism and for his obsession and his unstoppable passion, though perhaps this was not passion. His book, Icon and Image is written in the language of scholarship and he is a scholar for scholars and this book was not written for the African and it was not written for the people who produced the sacred art, the metal workers and the people who worked in the bush and who walked miles in the bush with a small piece of cola nut. It was not for them. He describes the rules of metal casting but not what is sacred and not what is special about the Yoruba people and it was a triumph of intellect over emotion. And what is sacred is that which is untouched by the thought of man and the thought of woman and what is called rational and sane and stuff like that. For what is sacred is the beginning of art and the beginning of creativity.

I can remember as a child when he came to the table in Lagos and this was the best place to see him and meet him. In his hand he had a carving, which looked like a wooden doll, and he was as excited as a young child with a treasure. He had come across a genuine artefact and he was saying: "This is not an imitation it is the real thing. This is not something you find in the market and this is not something to be found at the hotel." He was bubbling with an intensity I had never seen before as if that object carried the very human potential of his existence and in the body of this icon he saw something of his lost self and he saw something of his lost cultural identity. It is not him, but he makes it him and he makes himself into an object of himself and makes it his lost body and his original body and his Lobo, which is a character in his first book. And this dark objectified body is his body and both father and Ulli sought liberation through the "other."

Our home in Lagos – my father later moved to Lagos – was full of artefacts, which means things and those things were Yoruba figures and bones; and he tried to collect what is sacred and he tried to own it and he tried to build a culture out of his words and his ownership of these things. And how difficult it was for him and he was a man looking for his destiny, everywhere but not in the places where it mattered and not within his own soul and he was even searching in the soil for his own body. And in this magisterial book he left out the voice of the other and there is no voice, as in Other Leopards, save his own.

And he studied the African mask and the bronze figures of the Yoruba culture and with the African sacred "dolls" and he helped other writers such as the young Dennis Brutus and Jacob Afolabi and many others and he helped Ulli Beier with his art workshops in Oshogbo.

Chapter Twenty
In which I saw a Light in August.

And I would never have understood my father or my mother in any clear way unless I had come upon a book called Light in August. I was living in Bethesda at the time when this book came to me. I had already read Light in August as a young child; not really read it, but it was one of the books which were my father's books and one of the books I had taught myself to read with because there weren't any other books back then. I guess you could say or I could say that the seeds were sown here.

I was living in Bethesda and I had been invited to the house of Pat Daniel and she was having a party. It was a Saturday or a Sunday afternoon and I had walked up from the town which is where I lived: I had walked up from the town up through John Street and passed the old slate toilets place, the toilets that were no longer there. I had walked up the narrow and rocky road, which was not a road and was the one that the quarry workers must have walked up to the old Pant Dreiniog quarry. I passed the space where my mother's shop had been and I had walked up by Bryntirion and up to Carneddi where Wil Wandrin's house had been and then along the Carneddi Road by Siop Anne. Her house was just near to where I used to live in the old India Rock factory in Cymro Street though it was scarcely a street.

A woman at the party began talking about miscegenation and I don't quite remember why. I had never heard anyone using this word and she said she had been reading Light in August when she was at college and at that same moment I remembered being a little girl on the veranda, and it was one of those awakening moments when reality bursts into a dreaming world, which is quite the one I lived in. Dreams have to surface and live and die; so at this moment I was in the part of the dream that said you are reading Light in August by William Faulkner and this is your father's book. So it was that moment and that day that I decided to find the book again in order to release the dream: there is something quite honestly material about dreams and thought; the orange cover, the dry pages, the small writing which I could see and almost quite feel.

The very next day I went to the little book shop in Bethesda and I opened the door; it had an old bell on it and as it rung I saw that the sun was shining in and the light was pointing as a line to an orange book on the shelf. I walked towards it as if directed and I picked it up like it was mine, and my dreaming world had become real.

And the story of Joe Christmas and Mrs Burden is of course what I am interested in because I have never come close to an understanding of miscegenation as I have with this story and I am interested in these two characters because of the similarity to my parents. And this lead me to thinking about and formulating a kind of miscegenation mitosis, which is a kind of very intellectual way of putting things and I am apt to be very intellectual at times, despite my wishes to the contrary. Everything is about desire and its nature and everything is about sex and its nature and who can express human desire and who can talk and how they talk. Miscegenation – a strange word – that means race mixing and mitosis means splitting into parts and this is an underlying theme of my writing.

My father wears the mask of a white man though he is really a black man and what is important to him is thought and language and he has been raised to be like the image of the white man. And when your life is split between who you really are and the person who you want to become there is confusion. And the person he is, is mainly intellectual and white, and he says he wants to be a black man, but all the time he wants to be a white man because this is a more safe and committed place to be.

My mother said he had a chip on his shoulder. She said: "Black people have a chip on their shoulders," and there was much she didn't understand about his being in the world which was in some respects not at all like her being in the world. And my mother, by default was a black woman: he took up, as some white people do, all the whiteness so to speak. All the whiteness without sharing one drop: and she was by default a black woman. And my father sucked up all the whiteness and what that would mean. My mother, Catherine was in death the colour of white paste but in life she was what is commonly known as flesh or white or pink: her skin was transparent and you could see in to her bones and the blood inside her body. Her skin was definitely not black. My mother was reared for servitude and a life of serving rich people, her betters. And she was brought up in a home in Caernarvon, which was in the old Caernarvonshire, and she was raised to be a servant and a drudge and a menial and to not express her wants. And she had left Pant Dreiniog and she had left Carneddi and she had left Gerlan and Bethesda and the mountains and the rivers and the streams up on the quarry, which was her home.

And like my father, who she was, was decided for her and she was reared to feel the guilt and she was reared to feel the shame as poor people are expected to do. So many times she would say: "You are treating me like a dog," and she said it to my father and she said it to me and she said it to many people. A life of suffering was her piety and her place and her certainty, and to have a relationship with God you had to suffer and you had to have a life of suffering and she endured and she bore. She said: "Bear ye one another," and she did. There was little lightness, there was little fun and in her life with my father she played the role of servant and he was the white patriarch and she was the black menial with no identity save as being wife and mother. And if he was the head she was the body, his lost and alienated black body, his unexplored and his untamed Africa.

Because he was the head it was he who could express wants and desires and actions and advancement, and he could express omnipotence and his achievement and pleasure, though disembodied, and my mother could express her servitude and her willingness and the potency and plenitude of her human talents and her passion, and everything was upside down. My mother had a real talent and a real creativity; a real creativity because she lived close to the ground and to the earth and to the pain which transforms everything. And she transformed everything: every little broken piece of a plant she picked up from the road or any little scrap of cloth or any scrap of meat, she would transform it and make it into something worthy.

The art of life my father expressed was not a home made one nor a homespun one nor a particularly feminine one: it was a kind of framed one, a kind of fixed one that was hung on walls in galleries and places, and this is what the world calls art. And it was she who made him – she who made him a writer and a man, and years later he said of her: "I saw everything through her eyes."

And in another social context my mother might have been his social superior – her white to his black – but on the surface at least he was the natural leader and the divisions of the society were the divisions of the family and the divisions cut through the family along racial lines but in an inverted way. And my father played out the role well, and he looked like he was royalty or something with my mother behind and his daughters behind and this was the way we walked together.

There was a rigid and fragile quality, like china clay, which held this structure together and transgression between the roles was strictly forbidden and something akin to an apartheid existed, which is the nature of fragmentation; a white that must not mix with black and vice versa, and roles were sacrosanct and individual change a death threat to all, and any hint of difference or questioning was something wrong and a threat to patriarchy. And black meant menial sacrifice, endless compassion, and poverty and making do, and white meant privilege, it meant having a voice, it meant identification with father and much more: and for my mother all of this had more significance to her than her relationship with my father.

And I am a mummy's boy and I'm on the side of the family that is not to speak and the side with no head, and I am my mother's not-identity, the identity she dare not explore and in many ways she wishes were banished or dead. And also I am her stand-in daddy and a safe substitute for the real thing, and I am a confidante to whom she tells secrets on the understanding that I remain mute. She spoils me with extra food and she spoils me with extra attention: she doesn't want me to do anything and when I do nothing at all, she wants me to do something and I am caught up in her paradoxical needs. And she puts her anger on me and she makes her life my fault and she puts on and she puts onto me everything that she cannot put on her husband. My mother tells me how I will never work, and she tells me how I will never drive, and later she does her best to make sure I don't have a relationship with a man. She makes me a repository for her failings and she makes me a scapegoat for the pathology of the family, which is what she also does to my father, but in secret.

And my intimacy was with my mother and she did not want me to have anybody but her, and I was enmeshed with my mother. And the same antagonism existed in the family as existed in the society, and there is a division between black and white, though it is unconscious, and all of these things you are not supposed to notice, and I am not supposed to notice all kinds of things.

The main thing about the working out of power is that you are not supposed to notice that amongst us are those who think they are the best, and those who feel unrecognized, and those who are real. There is competition, and it is a competition for the image of the white man, who is the acme of society and the symbol of power, and it is the struggle between man and woman. And it is a fact of power and a fact of morality and it is a fact of colour and it is a fact of identification, and who can speak and who can't. I am a mummy's boy and I am not supposed to talk: talk is outlawed and I am not allowed to speak on behalf of the family, or anyone, or even myself. And food is split into functions and race was split into functions and writing was split into functions and sex itself and this is the mitosis and the miscegenation mitosis.

Chapter Twenty-one

In which I mention my miscegenation mitosis theory – where everything in the life is divided up as in a play.

She, my mother, does not speak, does not have a voice, except in private, in the family but not outside of it and I think that the play of patriarchy is to be kept a secret by the matriarch who must mediate his power. Small polite talk is permitted and my mother's voice is not heard and the other is not heard because there is no room for the other and the other is always negative. My father is positive, go ahead, kind of thrusting into the world and life and future and all of that. My mother's body is used and her ideas are used and the sexuality of the woman and the mouth of the woman is denied and she is the black woman and he is the image of the white man and the image of the black man and the black woman and the white man and the white woman are all bound up together.

I'm remembering my mother talking and when she spoke in English it was nearly always an affectation and part of her putting on, like Hedy Lamarr, a putting on, being posh and better. She put her two lips together as if her natural mouth was too wide. My mouth was too wide and she told me so, too big to eat food and speak. And my father would hold his lips tight and he always reminded me of a doll, something unreal and I found that very scary. A Captain Scarlet perhaps, who spoke English and kept his West Indian voice well hidden.

And once when I was twelve or perhaps thirteen I was standing at the front of our house in Wales and I was waiting and watching. And Mrs Morgan came by and she was one of our neighbours: she was Welsh and my mother was Welsh. They began talking in Welsh as though they fell into the words and so as not to be rude Mrs Morgan addressed my father in English and she said: "Hello Mr Williams nice morning isn't it?" and then he said: " Is it?" I watched in amazement and alienation.

And my mother was Welsh and she was from a little town in North Wales and she was Welsh and not English and each of her voices said something different and communicated something different of that culture. And each of these voices expressed a set of behaviours and cultural expressions that didn't meet and didn't want to and I could see the want that didn't want. I didn't know where to be, with whom and she, my mother was Welsh and she was always trying to be English and when she was lost she became Welsh and Welsh was the language of her sensuality and her feelings.

A chasm lay between them which neither seemed able to breach and this was the mitosis I am talking about and it was a chasm of a lack of closeness and understanding and fear and power and defence and the politics of colour and race, all the things that make us human. My father's charm fell away as he defended himself, and my mother's words are friendly and familiar and his are distant and cold, and he is not accepting this Welsh woman and she is not accepting him and they were speaking to each other across the separate worlds and not communicating. My father seemed rude and my mother seemed friendly but in this war of the worlds, she has her ally with her, for she was Welsh and he was a stranger and a visitor. And it was on her ground that he spoke, and Welsh was the language of her passion, of her anger and unresolved hurt, but English was where they met. And English was the language of culture and aspiration.

And my mother uses her language to get in the way of the meaning of the situation and it is the stuff of magic and mirrors. She doesn't know what she wants, her Welsh or her English at this point and she is caught with her obvious desire and she is ashamed of him and she is ashamed of herself for wanting the desire she doesn't want. And this is the man she has sex with and she is ashamed and she undermines him and makes him look rude in order to carry the shame of her feelings and she makes him the guilty one, the English one and the other one. She teaches me that man is responsible for sex and punishment and in order to create this real man, which isn't a real man, she manipulates him into being rude so that she can remain innocent and nice. And my mother will not and cannot own her own feelings and she transmutes her essence to him and then she makes him the repository of her frustrated desire.

And racial conflict is not a matter of colour, though everywhere it is: it is a matter of power and who has an image that is closest to the white man. Race was never spoken of in our home and sex was never alluded to but they were there like some huge presence. And it is strange to say that a black people can be racist which is hating blackness but I am sure that I grew up to hate blackness and to be as much as possible like that omnipresent but absent white man. I am quite sure I was brought up as some kind of white supremacist because I was like my father in some very particular ways and just as race was never mentioned I also grew up not being able to consider blackness or anything like that.

And when I was going to the big school my mother shocked me with trying to buy me a bra and I didn't want to be at all sexual because she had already made me like a boy, like my father and now she wanted me to be like her, a white woman. For myself I wanted none of it, not the thing she called a roll on. She said: "You have to wear a roll on to hold in your belly." But I was as thin as a post might be and I hated my mother. The trick is not to mention black in any shape or form and then if you didn't mention it, it wouldn't be there and if you did mention it you had to say how proud you were or something like that as another way of not talking about it. And if you gave the impression of claiming this image then everyone would think: "Ah great," how nice or how positive or something. Of course this is much the same as sex, which like race, is the thing people are thinking about but never saying.

My mother was insistent on this kind of innocence and it was her greatest obstacle and her greatest failing, but it was also the greatest obstacle of my father who was an innocent white man though he was a black man. My mother was pure and clean and that was the person she tried to be but this person she tried to be was not the person she was or all of the person she was.

My mother's white skin makes her different to my brown skin and my brown skin makes me different to my father's dark brown skin and all the time my mother is making me like her. My feet are so big and my hair is different and my feet are different to her image and my bones are different. And I do not want to paint my body white because it is not white and I do not want to paint my body black because it is not black. And how difficult it is to stay in the body and not be a slave to thought.

My mother always said that the trouble with society was that women could be bought and she often said the same incomprehensible thing to me. She said: "Women can be bought in this society," and she would say: "And what happens when the penis comes down?" And when she was angry she likened me to him and she needs his badness, the one that isn't her own and she needs to transform this badness that isn't her own. And she puts her dark sexuality on him and he does the same to her.

Race was divided and power was divided and talk was divided and so was food and enjoyment of life. There was a hidden tyranny that limited her life and limited it to certain fixed boundaries and this was a tragedy and I am asking myself is this something that men do to women and is it something that my father did to my mother or was it just something they fell into because of the wider culture? And there is no doubt that my mother was oppressed and held within certain boundaries and that she couldn't express her life and my father could not express his life. And she also held herself in tight boundaries, as did my father.

Somehow she had lost herself, and her desires were not real and my father's desires were not real. And this I suppose is what

Freud was saying about how we are alienated from ourselves, and my mother and my father were alienated from themselves. And nowhere is this alienation more potent than when my mother is preparing food. She washes up alone and she prepares food alone and no other person can participate. She nibbles and eats in the kitchen and so she remains unblemished desire – the desire she doesn't want. And when she eats at the table she puts a few morsels in her mouth as though she were not eating and the person who was not eating was an innocent child.

And when she brings the food to the table for my father she somehow manages to leave herself behind in the kitchen and she leaves her enjoyment in the kitchen. And her food was like eating love and to wear the clothes she darned was like wearing love – at least to me. To wear the clothes she bought for me in the charity shops was like wearing love and she had a great capacity to love and serve another human being and make that other human being feel or be at home. And home was what she wanted and home was what he, my father wanted; but it was a psychological home he wanted. And home is what every one wants though they don't always know it.

And in Africa if she fried a banana or a plantain she would transform it to a thing of beauty and she would buy the cheapest bones of meat and transform them into a meal of beauty. But when she brought that food to the table where food might be enjoyed she was absent and she would be rushing backwards and forwards to the kitchen and back again and she would not enjoy what she had prepared. And there was some kind of oppression or inhibition or rule, which forbade her entering the world.

And the table was where chaos met structure, body met mind, layers met lines, creativity met rules. And the table of the lord was how to hold your knife and fork, it was laying the table correctly and it was English and not Welsh. And the table was mouths and eating food and how to eat food and do not open your mouth and all of that.

The table was where she revealed herself as servant and father is master and my father was stiff and he is master in this world and he sat down to a ready made meal and he would eat it and he would never cook. And this was a metaphor for slavery and there was no please or thank you or that was a good meal and my mother ran backwards and forwards to please my father.

And one time when we were in Africa, my father was working in Lagos then, he bought a crate of Guinness for himself. He put around five bottles in the fridge and he brought one to go with his midday meal. At the table he would break a raw egg into his black drink and the black liquid would slip down his throat until I would see the round egg shape there. And I said to him, what about mummy? I said: "What about mummy?" but there was no response.

For food and talk did not mix. There were the rules of eating and she said how to use your knife and fork, and she said that when you went to the Inns of Court the barristers had to eat an orange with a knife and fork. Funny things like that. At the table she said: "Pass the salt," which is 'halen' in Welsh, and she said: "Use your napkin," and she said: "Take your elbows off the table."

And in Wales she did all the shopping and she did all the cooking and she controlled the world of appetite because she could control no other and she could not determine her life because it was bound up in the other and in doing for the other. It might have been a metaphor for slavery and my mother was my father's dark continent and she was an object in his world and she had no say of her own.

She was not a subject for her subjectivity had no validity except in the way that it was good for him. And the boundaries of this were what is public and what is private and my mother lived in the private inner world and my father lived in the outer world. My mother was a woman and she lived like some character in a private world and even when my father left she continued to live in this private world.

Occasionally she would let me do some shopping and that was my introduction to the woman's world.

And the public world must remain impersonal because it is a man's world and one must not be personal in the man's world and one must not be individual and one must not speak of feelings or the memory of having a body. And it is hard to know where this rule comes from, this oppression and this breaking up and abandoning of love. It was of course also something my mother agreed to and colluded with. On sea journeys she was continually sending food back for it to be cooked properly, and she would have to go into the kitchens and show them how to do it; she couldn't stand food that wasn't prepared by her. And once when this arrogance went too far, when she was very old, she claimed I was poisoning her with the food I prepared for her.

And my father: He approached the table like he was a character in a play, a play of being a white man and he was all stiff and formal like he knew what to do and what to say if he was introduced to the Queen of England or invited to the Guildhall. And this image wasn't him, but all the time it was him. And he would walk into the dining room and the table would be laid for him and the food would be prepared for him, as head, as godhead and his manners were impeccable, perfect and that was the whole problem, this perfection.

Ritualistically, he would sit down and place his napkin on his lap or on his neck. It was damask and perfectly ironed and he would wait in silence.

And at the table my father was showing and he could be seen and what could be seen was his face. And when he was seen, it was a whole mess of rules. He always turned his fork to eat rice, in his left hand. Turning forks was quite forbidden unless it was in the right hand. My father turned his fork in the left hand and piled up his white rice so high. Then he would pat the grains with his knife in his left hand and he would pat them and pat them some more. No loose grains could fall off and not even a

129

single one, and this collapsing of grains was quite disallowed; and he piled it so high and then he would tilt his head to receive this piled high rice and every mouthful was prepared and planned and executed in this style.

Chapter Twenty-two

In which my mother was a very religious woman and in which my parents leave me at home alone one summer and food comes each week in a box from Liptons.

And many people were converted at the Capel Jerusalem which is 'Jerusalem Chapel' in English. And I always felt this was significant and sometimes I imagined I saw something of this spirit; like when I saw the children run in the park as though they were re-enacting this same past. I remember someone telling me that people would rush around the valley in groups and there were spontaneous fires, and I always thought that spiritual places retain their spirits in some strange and mysterious way. And this place of Bethesda was one of these places, as though the past wasn't the past at all and that the stories still hung there like the branches which stooped down over the afon, which is 'river' in English.

And when she was a little girl she was part of a rich culture of religion and she was a Calvinist Methodist and the Home where she was brought up was a Calvinist Methodist Home. And some of the people who began this religion were called Griffith Jones and Howell Harris and in Llanddewi Brefi was Daniel Rowland who was a wonderful orator and my mother spoke of these men. And I always like to listen to Welsh hymns and one of the people that wrote hymns was William Williams, Pantycelyn.

And when we came from Africa the Reverend Hamilton gave my mother a brass nameplate and on it were marked the name Beiteel, which means house of god in Arabic and this was the name of our new house. I went to school at Craigydon and I sang all the hymns in Welsh and I went to Sunday school on Sunday at Llanrhos church where my sister Janice would one day marry Mr William Housely of Llandudno.

And my mother spoke of grace and how only god could give grace and she made everything she did her religion: her sewing, her cooking, her words, her patience and even her rage. And she was fond of making pronouncements on the fall of man. She read the bible and the bible she read was not the Welsh bible, but the one that Lynette had given her all of those years before. It was soft and black and it had wrinkly pages and some of these were torn and they had been repaired with sellotape.

Occasionally she brought lonely and lost people home for tea and that was a bit scary; but when the Jehovah Witnesses came to the door she would ask them to help her. She would say: "How about coming in to help me with the washing?" and she would frighten them away. And she told me that one of them had called her the whore of Babylon but I don't know if that was true.

She loved to read the gospels and these are the gospel of St John and the gospel of St. Mark and she would read all of this to me and I would sit and listen to her, though many of the times I was full of resistance and dislike for her and her bible, but later I became very interested in the gospels myself.

In the summer of 1965 my father came home to Wales and he said he had been invited to the University of Uganda at Makerere. He said: "I have been invited to a University at Makerere and I will be going there with your mother." But actually he wouldn't have said any such thing: he would have informed my mother and made her say it. So she said: "I will be going to Makerere with your father and you will be staying here in Wales and you will be fine because I have left you a list and there is money in the bank."

And she said: "You all look after each other and I will be back in..." I don't recall how long it was, whether it was six weeks or it was three months. It sounds odd now but it did not seem at all unnatural then, like it was nothing new and it wasn't the first time we had been left to our own devices and it wasn't the last. I think it was the way we lived and now it was as if we were the parents and they, my mother and my father, were the children out for a holiday.

She, my mother, left us a list for a shop called Liptons, which was a supermarket in the main road of Llandudno that before had been a cinema. A box was delivered each week and in it was a large box of cornflakes, and many tins of sardines, which my mother loved and there were pilchards in small red tins and white soggy bread and Stork margarine and Welsh butter and Heinz tomato ketchup and eggs and bacon and tins of beans and tins of tomatoes and dry rich tea biscuits. A large box, I can remember the shape of it and how it was used afterwards to play in or as a receptacle for the huge amounts of dry but un-ironed washing.

And my sisters were called Beatrice, Charlotte and Evelyn and we spent the summer playing on the beach at Craigydon. My sister Janice was already married to Mr Bill Housely of Llandudno. We spent the summer at the Floral café, which was tucked away down a back street and which is now an Indian restaurant and where we found some more parents and we spent a great deal of time at the fun fair and on the beach. Mrs Thomas looked after us and cooked chips for us and cared for us. My mother went to Uganda and my father went to Uganda and my mother had said: "Your father has been invited to be a Visiting Professor at Makere University," and she was very proud because they were going up in the world and not down into the world of children. They went to London where they took a plane to Uganda and they spent the summer there and not in Wales. And it was there that they must have met Mr Paul Theroux who was the reason I wrote this book.

Chapter Twenty-three

In which Llandudno was a much quieter place back in the sixties and my father dances a mighty twister and in which I visit my father in Surulere in Lagos.

My mother was responsible for Other Leopards: she was spiritually responsible as a mother of creativity is: she was responsible in a way that he was not, a way that only females are. And she was responsible for him being called a writer, though it was she who was the writer. And when my father was in Uganda he began a book called the Sperm of God and this definition came from my mother and not my father. I could always tell which words and sentiments came from my mother and which were my father's. It is hard to say which of your parents is which because they come in a package together but I can say that my father could not write without my mother, because she was the ground he wrote from and the mirror that reflected him.

And Llandudno was a quieter place in the sixties and there were not so many cars and not quite as much shopping, as people today are quite mad for shopping. I remember Brookes's shop where they sold school uniforms and thick green knickers and stockings and tights and I remember Mrs Brooks and her daughter, Pam Brooks. I remember the Gubay brothers, Albert and Robin Gubay, who used to shout outside his café. He shouted: "Two eggs if you are good looking!" and his brother stood outside the Oriental Stores and the window was crammed full of binoculars. I remember Madoc Street and Dave the Jew's shop and the donkey jackets and boots he sold there and I remember the bookshop where all the children bought bars of toffee candy and I remember Billy Mac's on the corner and Kirby's where I went to buy Rakusun's noodles in a yellow box. I remember a black woman working at the station and she rode about on a bike. And I remember Woolworths and Marks because it was the fashion then to have counters. Upstairs in

Woollies it was jammed with colourful inflatables and lilos and things: my mother would take me to Marks and she would remove the clothes from the cellophane wrapping and then throw the garments in an untidy heap on the counter. I hated her for this too.

My father came home again and he was still probably in the process of leaving my mother and I was aware of goings on though I had no idea of what was going on. He was writing another book or if he wasn't he was hiding in his room: he must be writing the book or making notes for the book which people are now saying he didn't write in Wales. And the book he is writing or not writing is called the The Third Temptation, which is a short book based in Llandudno, though I did not know this then. All I know is that my father was back and that he was in his usual place in the bedroom.

And all the places in this book are recognisable places to me, because they are the places where I live now and where I rode on my Palm Beach bike, which he bought for me because I passed the scholarship which wasn't a scholarship, to the big school which was called John Bright's. And some of these places are called Chapel Street and The Oriental Stores and Woolworths. And in the book he talks of living on the edge of a field which is where we lived back then in Maenan Road and this is where his character Bid lives which I can only guess is based on my mother, who once more is at the margin of his writing as she is in Other Leopards.

That summer The Byrds sang "Hey Mr Tambourine Man" and the sounds wafted like warm air across the town. And Elvis or someone sang "Joshua fit the battle of Jericho and the walls came tumbling down" and the hero in this book is called Josh and his world is about to come crashing down. Josh was also the nickname of the Scripture teacher who lived next door to us. That summer I asked my father; I took the frightening step of asking him if I might have some money to buy "I can't get no satisfaction" by the Rolling Stones and he was quite charming about it, though his charm was just about as scary as his rage. But that music gave me a rare insight because I saw that my father loved that music and it seemed to speak directly to him and he was doing a mighty twister right by the back door. Then for once I saw my father looking a little happy and having some fun and he came out the house into the yard and he danced a little.

It is hard to say what this book is about which is set in Llandudno because the meaning is veiled and the meaning is hidden and he is still putting the female down as he does in his other book while speaking of human violence in a very matter of fact way. The book is thin and it is white with a red abstract design on the front and inside the front cover it says To Miles, and Miles is his son by his new wife who is called Mrs Toni Adenle and I don't know of her other name, but she is not my mother.

And the main character is still looking for that elusive self which is himself, and the characters are all aspects of himself that he is exploring either consciously or unconsciously. Myself, I think the story is about a meeting with his new wife to be, right in the town of Llandudno where he is visiting. And the reason I think this is because Mr Bill Housely told me so.

The book is like a kaleidoscope of reflecting images in which he sees his own fragmentation. And the hero of the book he is now writing is again himself who is Josh who is my father who is still looking for a place in society and in Wales he cannot find himself and it is a book about relationships and the relationships he does not have. I have heard that his new wife came to visit him in Llandudno and I believe that this is what the book is about.

And I don't think my mother knew that and I didn't know that. And this book is a cover up to all that he does not say and all that he does not do. And my mother is waiting in the

136

background and she is unaware and she is still unaware of my father's philandering which are now not her father's but her husband's.

I have heard that when he came to Wales he looked in a shop window and saw himself and he saw what others saw and he saw his blackness and for the purposes of this book he erases self and he objectifies himself and makes himself into a stone. He cannot see himself in Wales, though others see him. Or rather he can see himself, the self he doesn't want to see. And the self he doesn't want to see is his black self.

And he is a Victorian and Llandudno is Victorian and he sees his Victorian black self. And he makes himself all the characters because he is in a magical spin and he cannot face himself and he shrinks from view and his feelings of loss and he doesn't know where he belongs. And there is no mention of blackness because he cannot mention blackness in a white country, though in his Other Leopards he can mention what it means to be black.

And he is in a kind of spiritual wilderness like Pincher Martin, isolated on an island and his voice is forever painful and inaccessible and fragmented and like a kaleidoscope. Or he is like Pinkie in Brighton Rock. And his human pain might have been more preferable but he cannot tell it and he doesn't see its significance in the integration of his psyche which he portrays as a kaleidoscope of colours and reflections. And Josh and my father are isolated and voiceless and they inhabit a closed world of an autocrat where there is no other.

My father moved from Ibadan to Lagos and he went to work at the university and he had a new house in Surulere, which was not a house but a ground floor of a house. Upstairs lived an African family and my father lived downstairs. And sometimes I could see the African family pass the doorway and sometimes the little boy from upstairs came to sit with us. And one time he sat at the table and he said: "My mother said I can't eat food with you; but I can eat toast."

The Lagos flat was full of 'artefacts', which means 'things' in English, and they looked like black dolls to me. Most were made of wood and some were in pairs and some were not. And the ones that were in pairs are called ibejis, or twins; and some had brass rings on them and some had elaborate carvings and some had colourful beads on them and some had cowries. Some of the artefacts were masks and some were not.

My father went out to work at the University and I never saw it or knew what it was like. And I walked with my sisters through the crowded streets and over the bridge into the city of Lagos. There were so many people walking right in the middle of the road and between each car and in front of each car. And many of the people were children and they had trays of things for sale. And the things they sold were little fried cakes and matches and slightly green oranges and tins of Tomapep and groundnuts. I remember staring longingly at the huge advertisements for 7up and Fanta as I was terribly thirsty but I didn't have any money.

Occasionally my father took us to Bar Beach where my father said the government held public executions and he described the black edged invitation cards that were sent out to people. I didn't speak to my father and he didn't speak to me. I have a poetry book he gave me and I used to have a children's book called Roof Top World. And once he wrote me a letter with a picture of a man doing limbo in an African club and this is all I have, though I have the father that is in me.

And it is hard to be compassionate towards such a person and it is hard to redeem what is good. I didn't know him and he didn't make himself known. He was a man with an obsession and one of his main obsessions was about iron and why Africans have sold their brothers and their children into slavery and this is a question which bothered him throughout his life. But this obsession was a thing of the mind and not so much an interest in people. And I have a letter and this is what he said to me, he said:

> *"Most importantly for you is that the slave trade was founded on what I have called iron hunger amongst West Africans. This is a discovery that belongs to you since it was made by me."*

And he was saying that this legacy was a property of mine because it was a property of his.

And it sounds as though he is making Africans innocent of such barbarity and he was saying that the black man was liberating himself through the smelting of iron. And it was human greed and desire that gave slavery its purpose and iron was the outward expression of this desire and iron was a metaphor for this desire. And my father's desire was psychological and he wanted to free himself from the iron, but I think my father was the iron man: he was hard and intractable, a wall of intellect and he wanted to understand the iron hunger but I do not think that he saw that he was the iron.

For the white man had traded iron for human flesh and the black man had sold his brother.

And my father traded his "dark daughter" for the iron of intellectual rigour and he traded his feelings and his feminine for this iron. And desire both liberates and incarcerates and it was not the iron but the language of the white man, the most intimate gift of words that liberated and incarcerated him. And language and words were at the very heart of slavery and it was used to subjugate and it was used to oppress, and my father talked like a master; when he wrote his books he wrote like a master, and the house of his language was more like a castle with no windows and no doors as a Welsh castle is. And his castle was armour plated and he was the iron-man and the language he spoke was not a language of affection, nor was it the language of the common man; it was the language of monument and edifice

139

and it was a language to communicate who was in charge.

I am sad I never really spoke to him and I'm not sure if he ever spoke to me and I do not remember him ever touching me or cuddling me. And talking and expressing feelings and being open was not what he did, and he was distant and he was impatient and he was often tyrannical. Once in the front room of the house in Surulere he said to me: "You will go beyond me," and I believed him, but many years later when I mentioned it to him, it clearly had no significance. And there was an unspoken rule that you did not speak to him and you did not criticise and you didn't undermine the power of that patriarchal voice.

And one time in that Surulere house he came home for lunch and he was all excited because he had found a new carving and he said: "I have come across this piece and it is a genuine artefact and it is not an imitation found in the market place or those sold to tourists at the hotel." And the doll was all rotted and covered with cow pee and poo or something. And he was bubbling with the intensity of a child as though the artefacts held the very secret potential of his existence and the key to his quest for belonging. And he saw the possibility of his own liberation. The black body was his body and he was a man looking for his destiny and he was looking in the soil for his lost body. But in all of this he didn't see the spiritual importance of the doll as a homunculi, as a symbol of the small and instead he made all his studies about what is big and important.

And that was the last time I was in Nigeria with my father because shortly afterwards the Biafran war broke out and all the Ibo people were being killed and all the children were starving and when we returned to Wales next time my mother said that my father was thinking of leaving Nigeria. She said: "Your father thinks he might be killed because he looks like an Ibo man." And she still didn't want to tell the truth about my father.

Chapter Twenty-four

*In which my mother hands out Christmas hats of different colours
and tells me not to resist evil.*

My father came home for one last Christmas and I didn't know
about his new wife then who was called Toni and I didn't know
he had another child called Miles. I was shocked when I saw that
this Third Temptation book was dedicated to Miles. And that
Christmas as we sat at the table eating Christmas dinner my
mother gave us Christmas paper hats and she said she had
chosen the colours especially and she was being spiritual and she
was often speaking in this way when what she wanted to say was
something else. And she was arranging all those paper hats
according to our nature. She said: "The one for you is yellow and
the one for you is red and the one for you is green," and so on
like that.

And I cannot ever remember having a Christmas like other
people had, with presents and all of that. I don't know if we did
or if we didn't. And I don't recall ever having birthday presents
or parties. And then this thing called marriage or family was all
over. One day my father got up and he left. I will not forget the
day my father left the house for the last time and I will not forget
the image of him leaving the house. He was wearing that olive
jumper and a stone coloured mac and he was wearing those
desert boots and I was coming down the stairs and my mother
said to me that my father was leaving and she said: "Your father
is going back to Guyana," and she said: "Do you want to go with
him?" then he went through the glass door and down the steps
and to the gate where there was a taxi. And he went in the taxi
and as the car turned he looked and his eyes looked all sad and
lost like a man who didn't know what he was doing. He never
even said goodbye or embraced me.

My mother was traumatised and she sat on a small stool, an
African stool we had in the sitting room. It was black and it was

made from one piece of wood and it had come from Africa. She sat there as if she had returned to her childhood trauma and she didn't really say anything as if she had become part of that piece of wood. And I was seventeen and I was not knowing what to do. And she was broken hearted for she had put everything into this man and in South Africa Louis Washansky was given a black heart and my mother took this as a spiritual symbol as my father might do with the doll in his hand and she said: "That man has a black heart and I have a black heart."

I suppose she did have a black heart because she understood something of the meaning of blackness and of darkness and of that feminine shadow or whatever it is called and she knew how to find refuge in the darkness of herself. Then responsibility was left to me, to be a mother, even though I was more of a father and I forced her and dragged her and I made her walk up the farm lane near our home and I made her walk up the granite mountain and when she came down nature had eased the pain.

And we had no money and my mother went to the Social Security for money and a man came to the house with a black bag and she walked the streets looking for money. And sometimes she found money and sometimes she did not. She went to work for Mrs Dawes who owned a guesthouse in Llandudno and she would leave the house and walk all the way into town and right through town to the other side and sometimes she would take the bus. And Mrs Dawes was a friend to her and helped her through this difficult time. I remember how we were so poor and how she would even bring small pieces of used soap home from the hotel and she would keep them in a glass jar for washing the clothes and for cleaning the floors.

My mother was forced to sell this Beiteel house, which was her first home, and she had to sell it because the bank said so. And after that she bought a small terraced house in Bangor on the mountain. She could not return to Bethesda although she needed to: she needed to go there to redeem her life and her childhood and her abandonment but she could not do this. And the sadness of my mother is that she had built something new or she was building a new culture but it fell down at her knees. To build a new culture requires a foundation and her foundation was not true and it was not strong.

She was alienated as she was alienated as a young girl and she had no place and she was Welsh but she was not Welsh anymore and my father went on a boat back to the West Indies and she never saw him again and I never saw him again and it was like her life had never been there with him.

And she began to talk about the theft of virtue and what she was saying I think is that he stole from her spiritually and not the words that she had given him, and not the time, and not the gift of writing that she had given him. He had stolen her essence and her passion and her very image and her sense of self and that was when she began to collect clothes and shoes and little bits of cloth and she was everywhere looking for an image that she had lost. And she lost her passion and she lost her voice and she lost her ability to do and create, not the passion for herself but the passion she had in working for others: but in all of this she did not give up on him or could not give up on him because of her contract with god, because she believed in god's grace and all the things of her religion.

And I became the mother for my mother, though I do not know quite how this happened. And some years later I found myself in Bethesda; I don't quite know how this happens that one person takes on another person's life and it may have been because I already had it, was already joined to her at the hip as people say. It happened because of the way I was joined to my mother like we were one person, which is a strange way of being. Lichens live like this. My mother and I had an odd relationship and later she said to me: "Your father wanted me to go with him and he wanted me and Toni and I couldn't go with him." And this kind of threesome was nowhere in my mother's thinking.

My father went home by ship and he saw all the black people there and he was shocked to be one of them and he was one of them. He went home to Guyana with the woman I know as Toni Adenle and their little boy Miles and he had many more children. I don't quite know what happened to him except that he went to live in the jungle and he built a house there like in the story of Thoreau's Walden Pond, which was in one of his books. I have a small photo of a man with a bunch of children and a tractor and I heard that the tractor was a gift from the president or something like that.

One day fourteen years later I wrote to him and he wrote me a note. And it is my understanding that fathers are meant to look after their children as best they can and this is not a matter of money, though of course this helps. But throughout his life he never wrote to me or considered my life or my mother, who had made him as he was. He stayed with his quest and his quest changed into a quest for an image for the Guyana peoples, an image that would unite them, but really he was looking for an image to unite himself. They were the same thing.

And he went on to begin all kinds of things in Georgetown and before he died he wrote a book on the prehistory of Guyana. I ordered it from the British Library and when it arrived at my local library there was an instruction not to allow the book to be issued: it had to be read within the walls so to speak. I didn't mind and it was for me a supreme irony that my father's last book was so precious I could not take it home. I smiled and saw that this book was another house, a castle even with no windows and no doors and the words were so scholarly and so long I couldn't possibly go in or even peek in. For a language is not just words, it is grammar and spaces and places for people to go in and out. Then I remembered a time when he came to Wales and set me some homework, and the homework was 'write an essay on communication.' And all that did was persuade me that I could communicate nothing and I couldn't write.

And maybe thirty years after he left Wales when I was seventeen, I phoned him and I had to work so hard to find his number and it wasn't simple and I was frightened of him still, since time does nothing to please fear. I rang him and he was at his office in the museum and when he answered he was as sweet as humble pie, but it was a sweetness I didn't like and didn't trust, a sweetness that was both an attack and a defence. And he spoke to me as if I was still a young girl and he spoke to the image of me as I was and I spoke to him as the image he once was and was perhaps still.

I asked him what he was doing and I don't think I had ever spoken to him. He said: "I am trying to fix my computer," and he was saying it like it was the most important thing. I asked him what he was doing and he said: "I cannot say what I am doing. You must ask Jenny, she has my bibliography." Except I didn't know Jenny and I knew that he knew that I didn't know her.

He was dismissing me but I wasn't going to be dismissed and I said that I was beginning to write and he began to be interested. He said: "What are you writing?" and I said: "I don't know what it is called yet…like a journal, perhaps?" Then he said to me something I will probably will never forget and that was: "You cannot write from a little cottage from North Wales; you have to write from real life." And once more he dismissed me. And my mind wondered about the meaning of this and I thought of all manner of things before I left it to rest. And one of the things I thought was that he was talking about himself and repeating over some thing he had said to himself some time before.

Then we talked about pioneers, who were Caribbean writers and poets and artists, because this was something I was also interested in writing about. And I mentioned James Baldwin and he got all excited about him and he mentioned a book called Giovanni's Room. And lastly he spoke of my mother and he said: "I saw everything through her eyes," but that was all that he could say.

I never phoned him again and he never phoned me. I wrote him two letters after I read Other Leopards but he wasn't interested to reply as if I was never his daughter. And on occasion he did reply and he said that my legacy was his discovery that the African was hungry for iron because it was his discovery. But on the matter of iron I thought he was mistaken.

And I think he made a mistake and that she, my mother, would have healed him and she herself would have been liberated: he would have been liberated not by what she said but through what she did – the sewing, the washing, the looking after children and all of those layers that make a woman and a mother. He would have been healed through his submission and he would have healed her and she would have been released. And it was the very hardness of the slate that would liberate them both.

And my mother moved to Bangor and she began going to charity shops and collecting shoes and collecting sacks and collecting all kinds of clothes and she read the bible everyday and she read a book called the Origin of Love and Hate and she read Krishnamurti and she read a book called Occult Meditation which I had bought for her. And a book she liked a lot was called 'Confessions of a Justified Sinner' by James Hogg and she still read her Blacks Medical Dictionary and she was always looking for new ailments.

She always said to me that there should be no resistance to evil. She said: "No resistance to evil," and she didn't understand her own religion because her religion always left her innocent and my father guilty. And she resisted her own voice and the power of her own place with him. She didn't stand up to him, she didn't feel the joy of resistance and she didn't feel the resistance within herself.

She cleaned the fireplace with her long reed brush and she collected and chopped wood on the mountain and she went down to the town and she talked to tramps and to lonely people like herself. She was poor but in her poverty she was quite rich. When she made her bed she was as the princess and the pea and if she could feel any lump or bump she would not be able to sleep.

Sometimes young men who were intellectuals came by the house and talked to her and she really liked that, and there was one woman who talked to her called Andrea and she ran a small communist bookshop. And the men were called Iestyn Daniel and Colin and Dafydd and these young men and intelligent men were like her own potential which she gave away to my father.

And I always encouraged her to write but she wouldn't; I think that writing would have redeemed her and saved her life as it did mine. And when my father wanted a divorce, she refused to divorce him and she went everywhere to find a person in law who would agree with her, that she was still married and she believed in marriage and she believed in god. Nobody did, but this didn't remove her faith, which was unshakeable. And she began to talk about society and how it was breaking down, and she said: "Before I die the tins will be rolling down the street from Tesco and people will no longer be able to talk." She said there would be a new language where people would talk in monosyllables and she used to demonstrate what that would sound like and she would put her thin lips together. But the tins didn't roll out of Tesco but it did get pulled down and now people speak in monosyllables on their mobiles so she wasn't far wrong.

Chapter Twenty-five
*In which I am at the paddling pool by the beach and I hear that
my father is dying and then he is buried as a hero.*

The day I heard that father was dying I had just returned to
Bethesda from a day out in Llandudno. I was cleaning the house
when the phone went and it was my son Morgan Joe, and he
told me that my father was ill. I didn't know then that he, my
father, was dying; all I knew then was that he was very ill. And
Morgan Joe said: "Your father has cancer and he's going to have
an operation."

I remember the day well; it was sunny and nearly summer, the
air was warm and I picked up the phone and rang my mother,
who was not yet dead and she was not dying and she knew
already that father was ill, very ill and she said: "Father is ill," and
she sounded glad and happy and relieved as if father had come
back to her; father had returned with a magical spell and a key
to awaken her up from her waking sleep.

I had been in Llandudno that day, and I was with Mary; her
father was also an artist, as mine was, and we had been down at
the paddling pool talking and laughing and quite near to where
I used to go as a young girl and near where mother was to die
and the same place where I was to visit her and the same place
where she had her first baby and where she was hounded down
by an angry young man, who was a soldier with a gun and her
first husband.

And that day was like magic as some days are. I was under a
spell; I felt myself magically drawn to this spot: a little girl had
been murdered there and it was a place I had come to on my bike
when I was a little girl. And the sadness and very heart of the
place made me fall, fall in love, or something like that. It was a
warm day in early summer and a warm breeze was blowing in
from the sea. Mary and I sat on the beach near the sea and close
to the Little Orme – there are two Ormes, the Great Orme and

the Little Orme on either side of the bay. We were talking in a psychological way about this and that and we walked over to a small shop and bought ice creams and only a few people were around because it was not yet summer and we settled ourselves down on the rocks. The mood was quiet and the air was warm and breezy and an occasional car passed on the road behind us because it was not yet the summer. I felt surprisingly rested and relaxed when I felt something touch me, which really wasn't anything at all. And I was startled and was awoken from my own reverie and I was thinking about the little girl that had been murdered because this was the place and I remembered what a lonely person I was and how lonely I was when I was a girl; not just lonely but cut off and out like my mother was and my father probably was and I felt sad in a gentle kind of way. And then I thought again about father and I wanted the image of him to live and die but wishing it didn't make it happen. So much of being there reminded me of him, father and not her, mother; the place that reminded me of mother was Bethesda. And Llandudno was my stand-in father and Bethesda was my stand-in mother and it was all imagination and not real at all. I was living in Bethesda then and Bethesda was my mother and Llandudno was my father.

And after I was touched I felt a great lightness of being and Mary and I walked along the beach and played games. I pointed to the houses, the big ones that overlooked the sea and I said, jokingly: "Which one would you like, which one do you want?" And she said: "That one," pointing up from the beach and then it was my turn. We returned home in her car and we went up Queen's Road and the house where Glenys Jones used to live and I couldn't help remembering how envious of her I was when we were both at school because she had such a lovely home and a father who had a small shoe shop.

We passed Deganwy and the Conwy Castle and Penmaen-mawr and Llanfairfechan and Aber and I returned home to Bethesda and that's when I had a phone call. And my son,

Morgan Joe, lives in Australia and he said: "Your father is having an operation," and he said that two of my sisters were going to see him. Straightaway I rang my mother who lived in a small flat in Bangor, but she already knew and was excited, because she had been waiting for thirty years for him to come home, in order to complete a story or something like that. Because he was the one. She said: "Oh, Denis is going to have an operation and he is having the best surgeon in Guyana." She woke up for a moment, as I had done that day; woke up briefly from a long waking sleep of waiting; waiting for an awakening to come from outside. And I didn't know what to feel or what was expected of me or anything really except I knew something of the father in me.

He was in Guyana and not in Wales, which might just have been a million miles away and it might have been because he was in that other world. And Guyana, like Wales is an old colony and I didn't go to see him one last time like I did with my mother; it didn't seem right to visit the man who was my father and who had left my mother and myself with no money and just a whole lot of debt, and it didn't seem right to think that there might be any kind of relationship with him, my father. I didn't know him, though I was him. He had been in England fourteen times, I had heard, but he had never once come to see his daughters or the woman who had made him, and when he was dying he had nothing to say as if I was not his daughter.

In London lived Miss Verna Williams; she was one of my father's sisters. He had others, who were called Eileen and Leila, who had already died. He had a brother too who was called Everard, whom he used to play with as a child and who also died of sickle cell anaemia. Verna was father's sister and she looked like him and a little Chinese too because her mother, whose name was Isabel Adonis, was part Chinese. Her skin was the same skin, her nose, the same nose, and her eyes the same eyes. And she would be at my mother's funeral standing not far from the grave and all my mother's daughters.

When I heard father was ill, I rang her and I said that I had some sad news about her brother. I said: "I have some sad news about your brother and he is having an operation for cancer." I didn't know then that he was dying, though I might have guessed. She replied by saying that it couldn't be true. She said: "It can't be true or I would have heard about it," and she didn't believe me and I said it again and again and she didn't believe me. But it was true. And my two sisters, called Evelyn and Charlotte went to see him and I couldn't because I was poor and in any case I did not wish to do so, perhaps through principle or perhaps through ignorance, and perhaps even through fear. I hadn't seen him for thirty years, though I knew that I was him on some level, which I did not then understand.

When I heard that my father was seriously ill I thought about Llandudno and how we had come to live in Wales in 1959 just after my youngest sister, Beatrice was born in Swansea and how we had stayed there for three months and my mother had given birth to her fifth child and there were five girls. I went to Sketty School on the bus with my sister Evelyn and we lived in a tall terraced house near the entrance to Cwmdonkin Park and there were tall trees in front of the house. And father had come to Sketty School in a dark tailored suit, a white shirt and a white hanky in his pocket and I was terrified of him, not just because he was black and the way he looked in the suit which was so smart. My teacher said I had to say good morning to him because all the other children had said good morning to him, and I said: "Good morning Mr Williams," and it was terrifying for me. The teacher was being kind and respectful but it was horrible and she, in her kindness, called me "coffee with cream" in the Sketty School magazine, which I didn't care for, though I was only a little girl.

That same time, the same summer, my mother bought me a red woollen cloak: she had come to Wales with a family called the Yules's who were our neighbours in Khartoum; they were a white family and their daughter Poppy was very white, and she had tried to prepare for our coming, and this cloak was huge and it was for a grown up, and it had a black velvet collar and she had bought it in a second hand shop. I hated it then. She was pregnant and she didn't want to have her baby in Khartoum; she wanted to have her baby in Wales where she felt safe and she came on an aeroplane with the Yules's and she left us behind with my father.

Then we came to live in North Wales and my mother and father bought a house, which I did not like, and my father went away and we were never a family again. My father walked in the park with an elderly man called Mr Roberts and he had his hands tied to his back so he might keep his tail cool. I went to Craigydon School and then to John Bright School.

And I did not know what to feel about a man called father: I think he was still buried or denied or something like that and I no longer knew him who no longer knew me. I didn't know what I was supposed to do in a moment like this and how did I feel about a person I hadn't seen or heard from for thirty years. And he was in Guyana and it was a place in another country and a country I had never been in, though I could imagine well enough the trees and the long rivers and the old colonial buildings. In thirty years I had had two notes from him in response to my correspondence; he didn't write of his own volition: and in all that time he didn't write and I was forgotten to him.

Father died soon afterwards and my sisters Evelyn and Charlotte went to Guyana to see him, but I did not and many other members of the Williams family did not. Some thought they should: some thought they were the rightful representatives and others did not. And father was buried as a hero and not a supplicant and he was buried with full honours: I can only imagine that he had a wooden box and that the great and distinguished were present at his burial and many wise things were said and his many identities and his many selves were paraded in a long rendition of glory.

And his sister in London wrote me a few notes expressing how "we were sad" and "we are" this and "we are" that and I honestly didn't know what to say to this and I couldn't reply to them. She said: "We will miss Denis, and we are sorry he didn't spend time with us and didn't talk to his children." But I didn't agree with her, since I did not know him and I couldn't grieve for someone I did not know, though I only knew the father in me.

And on the matter of desire father's wants were allowed freely and without restraint and were those and more that were expected of a man, and as much as my mother denied all desire, my father affirmed it and this was a reflection of her denial. And my father had the desire of two people (or more), an enhanced desire you might say, which gave him the power and the identity to act and to own and to move. His wanting gave him the right to move and be heard in the world and there was no question of it not being so. Desire propelled him from this thing to the next – I want, I must go and I will do this and I know and I will be, and it went in a circular motion. His was a world of achievement, of art and writing, archaeology and anthropology. A somebody, a person who counted where a woman who is a mother and carried five babies in her womb and bore them, fed them and clothed them, took them to school and brought them back from school, made parties and cakes and cooked, washed, made ends meet was not a hero, in fact was a nobody who didn't count.

And my father was buried as a hero and my mother was buried outside the town of Bethesda and she was not a hero, though given her circumstances in life, I think she was heroic and perhaps my father was too, but I didn't know him.

And Mr. Ian McDonald, the chief executive of the Sugar Association of the Caribbean (Incorporated) at the Demerara Sugar Terminal gave a eulogy at his funeral. He himself was a man of letters and he had published a novel (or two) and wrote weekly for the Starbroek News in Georgetown. And he had been writing for many years and had known my father since 1969 when he left my mother.

He spoke of him, my father, in superlative terms to all those gathered around him; he spoke of his abounding professional accomplishments and he said he was overwhelming and creative and he said he was a great man. He said: "Denis Williams will leave a vacancy that could not be filled," and he spoke of the "archive of his mind."

And Mr. McDonald knew Denis, the man who was my father; he knew him when he went back to Guyana from Africa: no mention was made of Wales. Perhaps my father himself had not mentioned it: he said he used to send him books and magazines to the forest where he was living and that he never failed to thank him for his letters which he treasured, describing him as a "West Indian Leonardo."

Father was dead and his death wasn't a great loss to me since I didn't know him and my task wasn't to stand humbly and express his greatness; my task was restitution which is why I became a writer and not because I particularly enjoyed it or was particularly ambitious and not because of sentiment, though I came to enjoy it; but because my life depended on it. I needed to get to the truth of the matter and I needed to find myself, which restitution would bring.

And so on Saturday July 4th 1998 in Wales and in England, in Scotland and in Ireland, and other parts of the world, the Guardian Newspaper printed an obituary on Denis Williams for all to see; a half page obituary entitled Icons of Identity, written principally by Anne Walmsley and there before me was a photograph I had never seen of a young man sitting cross legged on a stool before a painting and in his hand were three brushes and the painting was of trees and a naked woman looking outwards. He is sitting before a painting in Guyana, half turned: it was British Guiana then; and I know it's Guyana because I recognise the tropical shutters that are used as windows.

When I look at his mouth I see my mouth and when I look at his nose I see my nose: he's serious and he's not smiling and in his left hand he's holding a paint stained rag. At the bottom of the article it says Denis Joseph Ivan Williams, painter, art historian, teacher, novelist, anthropologist, archaeologist, born February 1923, died June 28th 1998.

My mother wasn't in the Guardian; I don't think she was in any of the papers I had seen and she wasn't mentioned in his obituary or any other wife or child, as if he had gone through his life wifeless and he had gone through life childless. His wife and my mother was called Catherine and some of his children were called Janice, Evelyn, Isabel, Charlotte, Beatrice, Miles, Everard, little Denis and Morag and Kibilieri. Some of them I have met and some of them I don't know. My mother wasn't there, not even a mention, as if my father had gone through life making achievement after achievement without relation. I was angry at being ignored: me and all the other wives and children and the lives, which were the price of that achievement. And I thought about my mother's continual suffering and her loneliness and her being neglected and how my father had left his daughters to die and his wife to die and I remembered her and how she made him a writer and how she had made him so important. And I thought about her going to the Home and having to give up her first home.

Chapter Twenty-six

In which Auntie Maggie takes me as little girl to Bethesda and gives me a black doll and shows me the way home.

And when I think of home I always think of Auntie Maggie because it was Auntie who took me to Bethesda and she took me to Uncle Islwyn and she took me to see Uncle Glyn who gave me a two and sixpence and pressed it hard in my hand so I would not forget him. And it was Auntie Maggie that made me walk in the hot sun all the way up from Llandegai and up past the fields and the trees and over the bridge and by the wall so as I could see the river. And she took me to Cefnfaes Street and to Bryntirion and to a green shop which was called London House where they sold ice creams on dry ice.

And this taste of home was what Auntie gave me: I remember her house which was called Rhos Velo and her kitchen, which was not like a kitchen, but like a siop, and this shop was full and the pantry was full, like I had never seen. There were boxes of Cox apples and bags of things, full they were, and pieces of mam's bread paper and used bits of string and cake tins and real Jaffa juice and Horlicks. And this was the siop by the two quarries, where now there was only a space; the siop, the same with its Mellin's food and Rowntrees in the front window and all of that.

And it was the same with my Auntie Eluned's house, with her piles of papers and clothes and her old records and she was trying to recreate the siop. And it was the same with my mother with all her clothes and broken bits and pieces and poor Ethel and poor Johnny they couldn't do this because they couldn't remember. I went back and I made a siop and I called it Quarry View Stores, to live again and to heal that story and to honour the past and to honour history and her story for what those children needed was a home and they didn't have one.

And Auntie's house was like a siop and Eluned's house was

like a siop and my mother's house was like a siop and Auntie Maggie, she was always bringing bargains from Woods's, Colwyn Bay. And Auntie's house was home, instead of that space in the street where there was no longer a siop or a house. She loved the Black and White Minstrels because they were black like Bethesda and the Black and White Minstrels which she went to with old Johnny Willy – Ar Lan Yr Mor, which is Llandudno and to the Happy Valley and the minstrels were famous then and some of them were white men and some of them were black men. And the songs they sang were on everyone's lips. All the people with their fancy Victorian dresses and coats, and all the people later with the men with pink faces and white hankies knotted on their heads. And she was born Margaret Louisa Hughes and she was born in 1907. And my mother said: "She is ten years older than me and she didn't make a home for me."

And Auntie didn't do it and Eluned didn't do it and the small children couldn't do it. And each one that could, recreated the siop: and when my father left my mother, she recreated the siop for she needed to go back and start again. And I went back for her, because Auntie had showed me the way and I lived in a tiny cottage and I collected sticks from the woods for my fire so that I might start again. And Auntie Maggie knew my secret life and one day she bought me a black doll wrapped in bread paper and it was an ugly plastic doll with a boz eye. She knew though I didn't know what she knew and I didn't know what I knew because she was the one who took me there, dragged me up the hot open road, the very London to Holyhead road with its slate milestones, and she took me to Uncle Islwyn's and to Cefnfaes Street, and made me sit on the slate step, just opposite the space where my mother's house had been. She said: "Sit on the step and wait for me." Then Islwyn's wife came and said something like: "Bwyd yn barod," which is, food is ready in Welsh. I went in to that small slate cottage after I had been staring at the slate mountain, and I saw the parlour and I saw the piano and I saw the small back room and when we sat down Islwyn's wife brought me my dinner and she said: "This is lobscouse," or something like that, and it was so greasy and good with potatoes and cabbage and tiny bits of meat.

And I heard Auntie talking and the other people talking while I sat dreaming and I heard the doors opening and I saw the flicker of the fire and the logs in the slate fireplace in that small cottage; I saw all the mess that makes a home and the worn out carpet and the small pieces of lace and the glass cabinet and all the little specks of dust with the light shining about them and I heard the people go up the stairs and open the bedrooms to see the old quilts and the feather pillows and the feather eiderdowns and the old clothes, and I heard them mention, "divans" or something like that.

I heard them go to the bathroom and they must have noticed the bath scrubbed clean with Vim and the new plastic toilet cover. I heard Auntie talking and she was talking in a language I both understood but didn't. Then we walked across Pant Drein-iog and we went to Beryl and Ted's: it wasn't quite the same there: it was more of a posh cottage. And she said: "Wait in the garden," so I waited in the garden and I saw the quarry and I saw the town and I saw that there was a railway carriage in the garden and I couldn't work out how it got to be in a garden on the side of a hill.

Chapter Twenty-seven.

In which there is a great strike and a town built on slate called Bethesda

And in 1900-1903 was Y Streic Fawr which is the big strike in English and it was one of the longest strikes in British Trade Union history. The men who worked in the quarry could no longer tolerate the way Lord Penrhyn was treating them. And Lord Penrhyn had a row of houses built for those men who returned to work and they were called 'bradwrs' which is traitors in English. And some of the houses had written on them 'Nid oes bradwr yn y ty hwn' which in English means There is no traitor in this house.

And the quarryman's champion was called W.J.Parry and he lived in Coetmor Hall, which was near Coetmor Farm and near to Coetmor New Road and Coetmor Church where I walked with bob and my girls when my mother had died. Many women were hungry and many had to leave the town and many of the children were starving and the people were proud and resisted the power of one man. And in all of this they were proud and they resisted and they kept clean and well dressed and they kept their houses clean. And if I could speak one quality in my mother it would be her strength in resistance and endurance as was the very character of this town.

When my mother was a young girl she lived in Cefnfaes Street, which was a road that ran along to the Pant Dreiniog quarry. She lived in a big house, which was bigger than the other houses in the street. The roof climbed higher and the width was wider and the windows were wider and her parents sold food and groceries to the people of Bethesda. And when my mother was a little girl her own mother died and the shop went and then the business went. And my mother said to me: "It was all on the books, the business was in the books," and when her mother died she went to the home and the home was called Bontnewydd. I don't know much about that home because I have never been there, though sometimes I feel like I have. I once heard somewhere that this home was built with a gift of money from a man who used to trade with America and who had a shipping company.

My mother was a young girl and she was Welsh. Her hair was kind of cochyn, which is ginger in English, though it wasn't quite red either. I have seen an old photograph of a young girl with bushy curls, dressed in a school gymslip with pleats at the front and I guessed that this was the uniform of her big school in Caernarvon. In this photo are other young people and a young man with a small striped cap. And maybe this is a group on a day out to Penmaenmawr or somewhere.

There is something beautiful and mysterious about the town of Bethesda that attracts writers and artists. Some of them were called Caradog Pritchard and Peter Prendergast and of course there were many other artists and writers whose names I do not know. And there's a quality special there, which accepts them and accepts those who might do something and those who simply can't, a quality of openness even while there is bitterness. A quality of intimacy and closeness is there, like a mother, and there is still community and something of an old community whose very word was slate.

And my mother was a dark mother, even while she was a white mother, she was dark by default to my father and she was dark as the slate is dark and the cloud is dark and the hole in the earth's body is dark. The slate was hewn by men and worked by men but the slate was forever feminine. Some of the men were called 'mewn clofar' which is men in clover in English and some of the men were called 'hogia' r jacdo' which is jackdaw boys in English. And 'the jackdaw boys' was the name of the quarrymen whose future was black. And in that town called Bethesda the men quarried slate and they used to have to pay Lord Penrhyn for the privilege and they blasted the rock and they mined the

160

slate and the men cut the slate into layers and into all different sizes. And the pieces of slate were given special names according to their sizes, and they were called singles and doubles and double doubles and double double doubles and double double double doubles. But the name double doubles was changed to ladies and double double doubles was changed to countesses and double double double doubles was changed to duchesses. And even bigger slates were called marchionesses and queens. And there were two quarries or even more, and one was Pant Drein-iog and the other was Penrhyn and one was on one side of the valley and one on the other. I don't know where the others were. The quarrymen had velocipedes, which were called ceir gwyllt in Welsh. And the Penrhyn quarry was the wealthiest in Britain in 1765 because the Penrhyns had made lots of money from slaves. And once when I was doing some research I heard that they, the Pennants were kind to their slaves and looked after their welfare, but these facts did not satisfy me.

In the main street in Bethesda there are no pubs on one side of the road and there are on the other. Some of the pubs were called The Douglas Arms and the King's Arms and The Llangollen. The High Street and the A5 were the same road and the road was built by Thomas Telford, and on the road are milestones – some are slate and some are not. And that same road went all the way to Kilburn, which is where I lived in Oxford Road in my first home. My mother never spoke of the slate, though she was made by this slate community, as I was. Her upbringing until she was six was in this community and her language and idiom was this community. And this little girl had been left behind and she never did quite find herself again.

My father never spoke of sugar or plantations or his background and he also left his boy behind. My father went back to the jungle but my mother never went back to Bethesda. I went back for her and I went back to be her and to redeem her. I was like father or I thought I was like my father, but I had to learn a hard lesson, which was to be my mother. I went back so that I could tell this story and make this story mine, and make this culture mine. And the culture I made mine was called slate.

When I was just a little girl of three or four I said to my mother, I said: " And when you are old Mummy, I will look after you," and many years later I did just what I had said even though as a little girl I didn't know what I meant or what I was saying. But when she was old I asked her if I was Welsh and she said: " No, you are not Welsh." And then I said: "What would it take to make me Welsh?" And she said: "It would take a long time." Then I said: " Well, if it is a matter of time, then how long would it take?" After a long while she said: "Ten years."

I looked after my mother, and in a way I looked after my father too. I understood him because he ran away from my mother and I understood what running away might mean. I was him, although I didn't know him. I had three husbands and he had three wives and I had to leave my family as he did, and I read the same books as he did and I rode my bike as he did. And I was an intellectual as he was.

I was successful in my private life as he was successful in his public life. I read his books and I even loved some of them though I never saw him reading them. The metaphor for my father was not sugar because my father didn't speak the language of folk. My father was hungry for iron, but it was iron that held him and restricted him and what he traded for and he did not speak a homegrown language or a low language or a slave language. The language he spoke was not was not a language for intimacy and not a language for sharing. The language he spoke was a defence against my mother and the writing he wrote was a defence against the feminine.

Words are not life but only about life. And his writing was a defence to keep her out, for language is oppressive as much as it is liberating and my father's house of language had no windows and no door and no back door or garden or flowers. And in

Bethesda there are many people who speak Welsh, more than anywhere else in wales and perhaps anywhere else in the world, I do not know. I went there and in my hand I carried a name, a name on a brass plate and on the plate it said Beiteel, which means house of god or something like that. And later I had the name carved in slate and had it decorated around with patterns and I did this for my mother though she seemed not to see it.

I went there and I went there alone with my children who were called Sam and Morgan Joe; and later I had two more children and they were called Catherine and Yemaya. I wanted to understand about my mother and her home and I looked everywhere and in all the streets and the lanes and all the places. And everywhere I went and saw my mother I saw my father and they were not apart. I went to the Carneddi School, which was my mother's first school, by siop Foster's and I went along Coetmor to near where Auntie Beryl lived and I went to Grey Street and Cymro Street and I talked to the old men and I talked to the old women and I said: " My mother was born here in this town and she lived here and my mother's parents had a shop." I said all of this even while there was no shop, just a space at the top of a rocky path. I walked up and down John Street and up onto the green that was the old pant Dreiniog quarry and I lived in Caerberllan and I lived in Gerlan and I even knew Wil Wandrin and Lewis who I called a bag of sticks, because he came to my backdoor and said: "Bag of sticks, bag of sticks!" I knew Hedd and I liked to talk to the old men, and I knew Griff with his dogs in Carneddi and I knew Harry who sold me his eggs. I knew Ceinwen, her sister and her mother, and the sweetie man, and the sweetie man's sister Elsie, and her husband, because my mother made him tea once in the garden in the Cymro Street cottage.

Years later I met him in Llandudno and told him my mother had died. He said: "I remember your mother, she made me tea and asked me did I want sugar." And then he said: "And when she brought me sugar I said I will have two sugars please and when I looked at the sugar, it was black!"

And everywhere I went in Bethesda I said: "My mother lived here in this town and she had a shop called Quarry View Stores by Pant Dreiniog overlooking the Penrhyn Quarry and my grandfather was called Johnny Willy and he was thrown out of the church. My mother's mother died in childbirth and my mother was brought up in a home. And that home was called Cartref Bontnewydd and it was a Calvinist Methodist home and my grandfather was thrown out of church (my mother said) and her family did not look after her and her brother and her sisters. " And probably they couldn't.

The children were called Catherine Alice, Ethel and Johnny bach. And this was my story and the story of my life and when I saw my Auntie Beryl who was my mum's cousin I said: "Why did no-one look after my mother?" And she didn't say. My mother left the home and I do not know how old she was then and she could not go back to Bethesda and she could not go home to her father who was called Johnny Willy or John William Hughes. He was living in a small slate shed behind No. 2 bread shop just behind the bread shop in the High Street, which was part of the A5 road from Holyhead to London. She said: " He got thrown out of the church because he had two wives in the village." She even took me to the place and showed me where this shed was and I saw this small building on two levels made of blocks of slate. It had two levels and behind it was just rock or slate and in front of it a tall building with a bakery called No.2 where you could buy huge bread buns called baps.

And she was right, everything she said was right and it was the whole story right there and the story never changed or altered and even though I spent my whole life trying to alter it, it was the same. And she was ashamed of her father and she carried this shame everywhere and she said: " The sins of the fathers fall on the daughters to the second and the third generation." And she put this shame onto my father, and she put it onto me, and everywhere, so that she could remain innocent.

And when she was a girl the town was busy and many people worked in the slate quarries and many people came to Bethesda to work. There were many pubs and some of them were called Llangollen, The Bull, The Douglas Arms, The King's Head, The Waterloo, and The Victoria; and alongside these pubs, which were strangely on one side of the main road and not the other, were the chapels, and there were also many of these. I don't know all the names but one was called Bethesda, like the pool in the bible, and one was called Jerusalem and there was a chapel in Gerlan and other chapels that I do not remember. And the town was busy and music was played for each house had a piano. My mother said: " There were prayer meetings and Sunday schools and literary evening and band practice."

And when the Revival came to Bethesda there were many converts and I have heard that people were rushing about in groups and bursting into song. And every house and every cottage had slate on the roof and the slate was hard and flat and sharp and straight and the slate walls divided the fields from the sheep and divided the rain and the wind and the snow from the home, and the slate walls divided the gardens from each other and the slate divided the fields from the town and slate was and is a morality of its own, for slate held in what is good and left out what is bad. And the slate was geography and history and economics and anthropology and psychology and slate was the very sacred heart and spirit of this town.

The End and another end...

And when I was a baby my mother called me Isabel which was the name of my father's mother and the name of a dark woman (though I have heard her skin was not dark) and my mother sent me out of the home with my Auntie Verna and with Gordon and Sheila and later she sent me out to Auntie Maggie and Auntie Averil so that I did not have a home and I had no place in it, which was the same as my mother when she was a little girl. I was my mother's lost girl and there was nothing for girls, she said. She tried her best to make me a boy to give me the intellectual potential of my father and the potential she didn't recognise as her own. She bought me Johnny shoes and she had my hair cut like a boy so that all the African children called me 'el walad' which was boy in Arabic. And later I learnt to go away on my own. When I was grown up with my own children she said: "You are not a wife and you are not a mother." She put her potential into my father so that he was successful in the world and he died a hero and she didn't. And I was her little man though I was a girl and eventually I went to live in a little cottage in North Wales, and I always had to be I to her and what she wanted but did not want.

And when I was a little girl in Africa I would sit under my father's table because I knew I was just like him but he was writing his big words and he did not notice me. And when I phoned my father he said: "You can't write from a little cottage in North Wales," and this explains why I am like my father and why I say I am like him, though I did not know him. He was a black man always trying to be white and he was always unhappy with the white man he was trying to be and he was always caught between the white man and the black man and this fact is never resolved in his writing or his life. And he doesn't find the voice he is looking for which is always outside of him, because he has also sent it away and he doesn't find the voice of the small house, though he does speak for the big house. And what he is saying (to me) is you can't write with a black voice, you can't write with a woman's voice. He is saying you can only speak with the voice of the big house and the voice you can speak with is the white man's. And he was always looking for the other and Mr Ian McDonald said at his funeral: "His death had made a void which could never be filled."

And I came to Bethesda because I was my mother's lost child and I had to do the job she could not do and I did the job my mother could not do and I lived in a little cottage just by the Penrhyn Quarry and then I lived in Gerlan and then in the town. My father could not find his little man because he lived in a little cottage in North Wales and my mother could not find the little girl she left behind. And I was like him because I am the little father, my mother's little father and my father's little man who he always ignored, and the little girl my mother sent away.

And my father can never find the black man by staying in the big house. And I was my mother's boy but he could never quite see me. And he could not see me because I was always in between – the between between defiance and compliance, the between between hatred and honour, the between between black and white, the between between masculine and feminine and the between between rich and poor. And it is in the dark feminine that isn't his and in the dark masculine that isn't his and he can only find the black man in the little house and in the small. And that is why I said to myself I am father come home, and, and, and…

The End

About the Author
Isabel Adonis

Isabel Adonis is a mother, a writer and an artist. She has been published in the *New Welsh Review*, *Urban Welsh*, *Just So You Know*, and the *Journal of Caribbean Literature*. She was the winner of Best Article 2002 in *Impact* magazine.

Born in Kilburn in north London to a Welsh mother and West Indian father, Isabel moved to the Sudan at age six and back to Wales at age nine, where she grew up in Llandudno.

As a writer she focuses on race and identity. This is her first book.